The Road to Reality

Along the way we must cross difficult bridges,
and only the Lord can show the way.

COMING HOME TO JESUS FROM THE UNREAL WORLD

THE ROAD
TO
REALITY

K.P. YOHANNAN

gfa books
A DIVISION OF GOSPEL FOR ASIA

gfa books
A division of Gospel for Asia
1800 Golden Trail Court
Carrollton, TX 75010
(972) 300-7777

Unless otherwise noted, all Scripture quotations are from the
King James Version of the Bible.

Second printing, April 1989.
Third printing, November 1990.
Fourth printing, June 1996.
Fifth printing, November 1999.
Sixth printing, April 2001.

Dedication

This book is dedicated lovingly to my wife, Gisela. She was the first who chose to walk this reality road with me. And, thank God, despite the tears and trials, she has never once looked back.

Acknowledgments

O ne is painfully aware that it is impossible here to acknowledge the many hundreds of people who have influenced my life and ministry over the years—and have thus had the greatest impact on the contents of this book.

The Road to Reality is more than a collection of thoughts gleaned from my spiritual journey. It is a result of leaders, friends and co-workers who went out of their way to disciple and instruct me in the things of God. I thank all those who took the time to confront me lovingly with the truths outlined in this book—and for those special individuals who modeled for me this life of victorious spiritual warfare. In these pages, it is my hope and prayer that the reader will learn some of the lessons taught through a host of spiritual mentors.

However, I especially want to thank those who were closest to me during the months of writing and editing this manuscript, William T. Bray and Robert Walker.

Special thanks to Heidi Chupp, as well as the many helping hands at Gospel for Asia, who contributed in countless ways.

Finally, I thank our faithful home team staff and personal friends who took the time to read and critique this manuscript at the many stages along the way. To God be all the glory.

Contents

Dedication 5

Acknowledgments 7

Foreword 11

Preface 13

Part I: The Deadly Dichotomy

1. Called to Be a Servant 17

2. A Deadly Dichotomy 21

3. Not What We Do, But Who We Are 29

4. What Really Is Going On? 34

5. How Long Will We Be Duped? 41

6. God's Purpose for You 46

7. A Lifelong Battle 52

Part II: Rediscovering Jesus Christ

8. No Pain, No Gain 61

9. Real Faith Doesn't Come Cheap 67

10. One-Way Ticket 74

11. Be Holy As I Am Holy 79

12. Battle Lines Must Be Drawn 85

13. At the Crossroads 90

14. Spiritual Intimacy 95

15. More Attitude Than Action 100

16. The World, the Flesh, the Devil 107

17. God Has Blessed America 113

18. Call to Missions 119

19. The Army of God 125

20. Get Involved Personally 130

21. Loving Is Sharing 136

22. Live as Christ Would Live 141

23. God and Riches 148

24. New Testament Simplicity 154

25. God Wants You 160

26. The Model of Servanthood 169

Part III: A Role Model for Our Times

27. Paul, A Dangerous Man 179

28. The Secret of His Life 184

29. Waiting for Orders 190

Foreword

Every once in a while God gives to His people a man who is qualified to cut us open, give us a diagnosis and prescribe a remedy for our healing. K. P. Yohannan is such a man.

This is not a book about missions, although the author's heartbeat for the evangelization of the world pulses on every page. This is a book about spiritual reality; about what it means to be a follower of Christ in the 21st century. It's a book about the spiritual condition of the Western church in light of the awesome needs in other parts of the world.

You will quickly discover that K.P. is a man of deep passion. He fervently loves the believers in the United States and Canada but is grieved over the spiritual insensitivity of the church at large. With tears he admonishes us to leave our fascination with material prosperity and the enjoyment of personal pleasures to turn to Christ with all our heart. That, after all, is the path to true happiness and fulfillment. K. P. calls it reality.

Here is a book that cuts through the welter of pseudo remedies for spiritual renewal and returns to the basics. The author is impatient with intellectual knowledge unless it translates into holy living and a single-minded determination to see the church around the world grow for the glory of God. And he practices what he preaches.

Every believer who is concerned about the spiritual life of the church in America ought to read this book. You may find, as I did, that at times his analysis made me feel defensive and uncomfortable, but in the end I knew he was right.

This book has the power to change anyone who is weary of half-hearted Christianity and is unafraid to take some giant steps with God. Through these pages K.P. will come into your room, sit down and share his heart. If you listen carefully, you will leave with "eternity stamped on your heart."

Erwin W. Lutzer
Senior Pastor
Moody Church
Chicago, Illinois

Preface

We lost it. Somewhere along our journey from a dead religion of laws and guilt, we modern Christians have misplaced the other side of grace. It was undoubtedly left beside the road with the best of motives. I'm sure that most of those who abandoned reality sincerely wanted to display the immeasurable love of God to a lost and needy world.

But we have failed to reveal the wonderful grace of Jesus we sing about with obedience in our everyday lives. Instead, we have produced an "old dishwater" kind of religion—that insipid, lukewarm faith that Jesus said He would spew out of His mouth!

All those uncomfortable Scripture verses about taking up the cross—discipline, sacrifice and suffering—somehow, they just seem to get in the way of our modern-day "convenience store" Christianity. We've been taught to serve up a watered-down gospel for so long that the real Gospel has become an embarrassment.

However, half a truth is no truth at all. Obedience must always be a vital part of our response to His love and grace. Faith without works is dead. It is time for us to find our balance again—to restore authentic Christianity before it's too late. Distorted, perverted gospels always self-destruct.

If I have any prayer at all for the reader of this book, it is that God will use it to help you take your first steps. The bridges to reality in our spiritual pilgrimage may seem a bit unfamiliar.

The road is strange to us. The disciplines of spiritual reality are "lost arts" to most modern Christians. But they have been tried, tested and proven by millions before you.

They are your only way out of the fantasy and illusion of so much that seeks to counterfeit Christianity today. May I challenge you to come along and begin a journey on the road to reality? Won't you venture out with us and journey into the heart of Jesus?

K.P. Yohannan
Carrollton, Texas

Part I

THE DEADLY DICHOTOMY

Discover the mystery
of why Western culture contrasts
so directly with the lifestyle
our Lord commands.
How have we divorced what we know
from who we are and what we do?

Chapter 1

Called to Be a Servant

How perverse and twisted self can become in its drive to be recognized and applauded.

Early in my ministry to native missionaries, the Lord had to deal severely with me in this area. Rather than send money from the United States to the field each month as we do now, I had begun banking the support funds we raised. I did this so I could take them to Asia. I enjoyed distributing the funds in person, but for a reason so devious I could not admit it to myself.

Of course I rationalized. I told myself I was doing this so I could inspect the work and be on hand to help train the native brothers in the ministry.

In reality, however, I hoped I would be met at the train by missionaries and received by delegations from the churches. I pictured myself being presented with garlands of flowers, the traditional Indian mode of showing respect and honor to important visitors.

Although I was careful never to show it, my feelings were hurt deeply when I was not so honored. My ego was disguised, but regrettably I craved this sort of attention.

Now I thank God that many of the native missionaries we sponsored were men of high spiritual caliber who couldn't be bought. They were faithful servants of the most high God who praised the Lord for our help but were too busy winning souls to turn out and greet me when I came to town.

"Don't they know what I've given up for them?" I asked my wounded pride. "Don't they know how important my support is to the future of their ministry?"

Telling myself that it was for their own good, I vowed not to send any more support until I could go to India and hold a training conference. Perhaps then I could explain tactfully their responsibility to me, I thought. How pious pride can be when it wants its own way.

When I finally recognized my problem, I was astonished. How could this have happened to me? No one could have been more aware of the grace of God in his life than I. Or at least, so I thought.

Born in a jungle village in one of the poorest countries of the world, I never wore shoes until I was 17 years old. I was shy beyond belief. I showed no leadership skills as a young person and was a sort of non-person in our village, always lingering out at the edge of a crowd.

But I did have a Christian mother, and it was her prayers for a preacher son which the Lord answered.

The Lord Proved Faithful

Even then, the process of preparation for ministry had been slow and torturous. But the Lord was faithful. One miracle after another paved the way. First came valuable experience with a team of young traveling evangelists witnessing and preaching in the villages of north India. Here with my own eyes I saw the power of God at work in the lives of people whose minds and hearts had been blinded by demonic powers embodied in the age-old rituals and religions of the Orient.

Next was the privilege of attending mission and leadership conferences sponsored by Operation Mobilization in Bangalore and Madras, in my own country, then at the Haggai Institute in Singapore. Finally came the provision for me to attend Bible college in Dallas, Texas, in the United States.

Plainly, all this was the Lord's doing and nothing for which I could take credit. Even the vision He had given me to awaken the church of Jesus Christ worldwide to the great potential of native evangelism, I recognized as coming from Him.

However, as I looked back, I could see how I had been carried away—in part at least—by the ecstasy of the vision. Or perhaps it was by my interpretation of it.

Night after night across the United States and Canada I was speaking in churches of all denominations. In my messages I called passionately on people to respond to our Lord's command to preach and teach the Gospel to all lands. I pictured for them the desperate plight of the people of my own country who were without hope and with no knowledge of Christ. I pleaded with congregations to give at least $1 per day to support native missionaries who undergo almost unbearable sacrifice to share their faith in Jesus Christ. I told them the cost to support those missionaries is only $1,000 to $1,400 in contrast to the $43,000 it takes to keep one traditional Western missionary overseas for a year.

Response to my message had not been immediate. Yet in an amazing way funds came in. Gospel for Asia became more and more recognized as a respectable mission and our program of native missionaries as an effective form of evangelism. As a result I began to receive recognition as a mission leader.

I Got the Point

Then one night the Lord met me and gave me an ultimatum. "If that's how you feel," He said, "I'll find someone else for this work. I've called you to be My servant, and the servant of My servants—not a boss."

I got the point. And with confession came the joy and relief of repentance and forgiveness. Now I could begin to understand the apathy of Western Christians and churches. Consumed by the bountiful provisions of their culture, it was difficult for them to comprehend the situation in the sin-blighted countries of the Third World.

Moreover, I could see that in some ways I had fallen into the same trap. With my physical needs provided for in America, I was attempting to dictate to my faithful colleagues in India how they should respond to my efforts on their behalf.

How I praise God for His goodness in opening my spiritual eyes in this incident—and in others which came later. Holiness, I discovered, is not a state of being, but a continuing process. Peter reminds us of this: "As he who has called you is holy, so be holy in all you do, for it is written: 'Be holy, because I am holy.'" (1 Peter 1:15,16 *NIV*)

Since that day Jesus has led me along the exciting road to spiritual reality that has many bridges. Crossing these bridges has not always been easy. In the pages that follow I want to share with you some of the lessons I have learned in the journey. Even more important is the exhilaration that can be ours as we see the Lord Himself on the other side of those bridges encouraging us as we give ourselves totally to follow Him.

Chapter 2

A Deadly Dichotomy

The stones of the church parking lot crunched beneath my feet in the freezing December air. It was my first Christmas in America—and I was as excited and bewildered as any two-year-old child at the wonder of it all.

I had never seen a Christmas like this before! In many parts of my native India, December 25 passes without fanfare. For my people, it is just another day of bondage to sin, suffering and death—the life without Christ.

You see, in most of Asia there is no Christmas. For billions of people, Christ still has not come. His name, His peace and His redemption through Calvary are not yet known or understood. Most of Asia has yet to hear the good news of Christmas—*that Christ came into the world to seek and to save lost sinners.*

On the way to church that night, it seemed to me as if the whole nation were Christian. Streets, stores and malls were decorated brightly. Thousands of tired-looking people were filling their cars with bags and boxes of gifts, food and wine for the holidays. Nearly every home had colored lights, decorated trees and even life-size manger scenes telling the Christmas story.

"How these people must love Christ!" I thought. "What a wonder to live in a country which is saturated with Christians, churches and the Gospel!"

Inside the church I touched the beautifully padded pews in awe and walked carefully on the rich carpeting. Even the altar was decorated in red bows for the candlelight carols we had come to hear. A huge tree stood on one side with a large American flag on the other. The symbolism of a Christian nation celebrating the birth of the Savior was new and exciting to me.

In the front of the church was an orchestra backed by a hundred-voice choir standing in the pyramid shape of "a living Christmas tree." At first, I thought it was a tree. But then I realized it was colorfully robed men and women forming the tree. One man told me that the steel scaffolding for the display had cost the church more than $25,000. I couldn't imagine that much money—it could build four or five village churches in my homeland.

I looked down at the lavish program in my hands and wondered to myself how much it had cost to be printed. Back in India, I had been involved in printing tracts for our Gospel teams, and I recalled that five cents' worth of tracts would give the Gospel to 100 people.

"But these people love the Lord," I rebuked myself. "I mustn't judge." But still the thought wouldn't go away. If this printed program cost only 50 cents to produce, that would have been the equivalent of 1,000 tracts. (And I suspected it cost more than 50 cents!) I thought of the native missionaries I knew of in Nepal and Burma working without enough Gospel tracts among millions of lost Hindus and Buddhists.

The rest of that first Christmas was still awesome and exciting to me, but the thought of those unprinted tracts haunted me. Why did these people who already had everything still need to buy more? Why did they send so many Christmas cards to people they hardly knew? Why did they eat and drink so much that they often got sick? And how, I wondered, could all this be done to celebrate and proclaim the coming of the Savior?

If even the very name of the Savior is still unknown to millions of lost souls, I reasoned, isn't this self-indulgence a strange way to herald the coming of the Lord Jesus? Wouldn't it be more fitting to proclaim the good news of His coming to those who've not heard rather than to those who've already heard thousands of times?

Enormous Self-Deception

Since that Christmas I have crisscrossed the United States and Canada hundreds of times, speaking to Christians. I have counseled privately with hundreds of them about their beliefs and lifestyles. What I have found has to be one of the most tragic ironies of all times. A tiny group of believers who have the Gospel keep mumbling it over and over to themselves. Meanwhile, millions who have never heard it once fall into the flames of eternal hell without ever hearing the salvation story.

Most Christians are living out that Christmas irony every day in one way or another. As individuals, their lifestyles often amount to an enormous self-deception.

Who they claim *to be* is disconnected from what they *know*, and what they know is even more removed from what they *do*. It is so unreal. It is a mysterious but deadly spiritual dichotomy.

A dichotomy is a whole divided into two parts. And we as modern Christians are living dangerously in this double contradiction of our beliefs—especially here in the West.

To choose deliberately to live in a world of unreality such as this is a disease or sickness. For a Christian, it is also sinful disobedience to the Lord we love. It invites judgment from a loving God who cannot and will not allow us to go on living forever in such hypocrisy.

The message of this book is a direct result of my first ten years of confrontation with believers in the West. Many nights, after preaching my heart out, I have returned to my hotel room bitterly discouraged, asking myself how this paradox can even exist. It has to be one of the great mysteries of all time.

For instance, as I was writing this book, another great missionary conference was being held where thousands were gathered from nearly every state in America. Most were raised lovingly in Christian homes where the Word of God is honored.

They gathered to consider the claims of Jesus Christ on their lives. Some of the greatest Christian orators of our time addressed them. Some of the finest musicians in the world played and sang to them. Beautiful films and videos portrayed the needs of a lost and dying world in vivid graphic detail. Hundreds of Christian organizations spent tens of thousands of dollars to present the desperate needs of a world without Christ. Mission leaders flew in from every continent to plead the cause of the lost. In addition, the participants themselves spent huge sums of money to come and be challenged, educated and informed.

What will the results of this enormous investment be?

Thousands stood at the invitation and offered themselves for missionary service. But if this conference is like past ones, the statistical chances of even a handful of them going to the hidden peoples is almost nil. Fewer than one percent of those who respond to the altar call will ever obey the Great Commission of Christ and go to the foreign mission field. Of those who do go, over half will not return for a second term of service. The percentage that will actually go to the hidden peoples of Asia, where two-thirds of the world's unreached people are dying without Christ, is so small that it doesn't show statistically!

As another example, I recently was privileged to speak to the youth group of one of the great evangelical churches of America. It is a model of ministry that would be the dream come true of any pastor.

These young people are exposed to the most balanced youth ministry possible. They have a full-time youth director, Bible studies many nights of the week, monthly socials, weekly fellowships, a gym and sports teams, camps, conferences, concerts, video tapes, audio tapes, a big library, full-time counseling staff—everything!

I looked forward to presenting to them the burden of Christ's heart for the lost world. When I addressed 350 of these healthy, well-fed, bright-eyed young people with the message of New Testament Christianity, the results were incredible.

With tears in my eyes, I told them of the lost and needy millions still without Christ. Many appeared deeply moved.

But when I asked for a show of hands of those willing to give their lives to Christ's service, not one was able to say, "Yes, Lord!"

Since When Is Obedience Optional?

Not one was willing to break out of that velvet cage of comfort and convenience to begin *a radical lifestyle lived from inner reality that affects the world*. Since when has obedience to Christ and His Gospel become optional to Christianity?

What kind of church, culture or ethnic group can produce a faith where obedience to God has become dispensable? This is the question I ask myself over and over. It's the reason why I had to write this book.

These examples are not unusual—just the extremes. I address thousands of people weekly when speaking in North American churches. Even in the best meetings, it is rare that more than one or two percent of the listeners will pledge even $1 a day to support native missionaries, let alone volunteer for service on the mission field.

This amazes me constantly because most believers in the United States or Canada could contribute $1 a day—almost without sacrifice. Yet that small offering can mean the difference between spiritual life or death for some tribe or village in Asia where no Westerner can now go with the Gospel.

This should ring alarm bells in our minds and hearts. Something is wrong when Christians don't respond to what is so dear to the heart of Jesus.

What's really wrong? How can we diagnose the causes or come to grips with this deadly problem in our Christian lives? I think it is best described as the dichotomy of the modern Christian.

First, *we modern Christians have divorced what we do from who we are*.

We have lost touch with our spiritual being or self-identity in Christ. Seldom does our spirit-man lead and dominate. We are content to act out a religion of externals, a lifestyle disconnected from the life born of the Holy Spirit in our human spirits.

More than 50 million Americans have become what is mistakenly called "born again." By this, they mean that they have walked the aisle to be saved from hell, find peace and joy, escape from guilt, please family and friends, find wealth, health and happiness, and get that preacher off their backs! But a religion measured in such superficial, external terms bears no resemblance to the faith of Scripture.

Jesus is "cool" now in North America. Being a Christian is a respectable, acceptable and normal choice.

What's more, it's free, instant, a convenience-store item. All that is necessary is to pray a 30-word prayer, sign a little card, or put your hand on the TV screen and you're in!

This modern Christianity is weak on the Gospels. You rarely hear an evangelist preach from Matthew, Mark or Luke. To do so would mean that the ego demands of Christ on His followers would have to become a central concern.

Thus, the false religion of popular Christianity does not ask us to internalize the passion and mind of Christ, to surrender our egos, lay aside our flesh, take up the cross and begin a lifestyle marked by submission to the will of the Father as He did.

We are also seldom asked to internalize the commands of Christ—to begin a lifestyle of sacrifice, service and suffering for the sake of our Lord.

We are not asked to love as He loved, walk where He walked, interact with the kind of sinful people He did, and live the life of self-sacrificing service which was His trademark.

But what about that vast network of Christian activities that so often preoccupies our hearts, hands and minds in the West? Don't our frenzied lives prove our piety? I cannot look at them without asking the critical question, "From where does this current wave of activism spring?"

Will it pass through the fires of judgment? Is it the work of our own hands and egos, or does it spring from the heart of Jesus? If your Christian service were to end today, would it make any difference in eternity?

Second, *we modern Christians are divorced from what we know.*

Until you travel outside of North America, you cannot appreciate the religious information glut in the West. Christians here are blessed with thousands of books, 24-hour Christian radio, conferences and seminars, concerts, video and audio tapes, television.

Someone has said that there are more than 1,000 commentaries on the book of Acts in the English language—but not 100 Christians living with the power of the New Testament Christianity.

All too often, it seems, we're willing to be students of Christianity rather than disciples of Christ. The fact is that most of us are substituting learning and information for practical obedience.

Nowhere is this more evident than in the world of Christian missions. In the United States, the focus has shifted to learning about the hidden and unreached peoples rather than going to them.

Probably no culture has been better able to fulfill that frightening prophecy in 2 Timothy 3:1-8. We are a people "ever learning, and never able to come to the knowledge of the truth." We are indeed "having a form of godliness, but denying the power thereof."

Never in history has there been a society with so much information about God, but so little real knowledge of the Holy One.

Whatever the reason for this lack of spiritual reality in the West, it cannot be a lack of teaching resources. We have shamefully hoarded Christian knowledge, preventing the rest of the world from finding out the truth—while not taking advantage of the knowledge it possesses.

Why Are We Still Spiritual Babies?

The question that faces us is this: "How can a Christian culture that knows so much truth fail to perform?"

Why do we have all this Bible study? Our Sunday school and Christian education programs? Our Holy Land tours and Christian sea cruises? Our camps, retreats, seminars, conferences, books, magazines, newspapers, cassettes and broadcasting? Why do we now even have Christian theme parks, family theaters and coffee houses?

Isn't the reason to be like Christ? Isn't that what we say?

Then why are we still spiritual babies? Kindergarten Christians?

Why is there so little power and holiness in our lives? Why aren't we manifesting Christ to our friends, neighbors, classmates and peers? Why aren't we incarnating Him to those across town in our own inner cities—and to the lost billions still in darkness around the world?

Chapter 3

Not What We Do, But Who We Are

It was missionary conference season. There are two of them in North America. These are extended periods of special church meetings, lasting about 13 weeks each spring and fall. During this time missions-minded churches carry on an old tradition that began during colonial times.

During these months I spend as much time on airplanes as I do on the ground. Night after night I find myself addressing crowds of faithful believers who support foreign missions programs.

It is always a time of intense spiritual warfare for me, and I battle discouragement from one meeting to the next. As I preach each message, the souls of lost millions tumble before my eyes into the eternal flames of hell. Yet I realize that for many in the audience, I am just a kind of spiritual entertainment for the night.

As I have made the rounds of these conferences each year, certain truths have become evident. One of the most devastating is the fact that the concept of missions has been so cheapened that many Christians in the West now equate it with fund raising. It has been reduced to just another appeal for money, similar to the annual budget campaign or the building fund drive.

I'll never forget the night that I first came to understand this. Before the service at one church famous for its generosity to missions, the pastor asked me if I would meet to pray with him and the missions committee. We gathered in a side room. But there was little prayer. Instead, the financial shortfalls and budget goals for the conference were discussed. Finally, just before we were to go on the platform, one of the men led us in a short prayer asking God to "use me and bless the service."

I didn't understand the full impact of all this until just before my turn came to speak. The pastor gave a stirring challenge for missions and then introduced me in such heroic terms that I winced in embarrassment. Finally, just as I was coming to the pulpit, he asked the people to welcome the man who "is going to help us give our best offering ever for world missions."

Suddenly, I felt as if he had shoved a knife into my heart.

In that one instant I understood that he and his missions committee viewed me as a traveling salesman. They had a big missions fund-raising thermometer set up for conference week. And now I knew the role they planned for me. I was little more than a hired gun who came to help them color in the blank space!

I also understood why—in so many churches—I could share the exciting, new opportunities we now have for world evangelism, and yet see only two or three people pledge to support a native missionary or Bible teacher.

If and when missions is reduced to a dollars-and-cents decision—merely another option for our giving—we prove that we have lost sight of the Savior. The test of our true affection is not how much we *give*, but how we *live*. *Missions is not something we do, but something we are.*

There is a principle at work here: *Self-centered Christians cannot and will not respond to Christ because they are not submitted to Him as their Head.* Dichotomized Christians have reproduced their schizophrenic personal lives in the corporate life of the body. Disobedient Christians produce disobedient churches!

Christ's Unchanging Mandate

Jesus has made clear the mission mandate for each one of us who claims to follow Him. He said that He lived to do the will of His Father; the fields of lost souls were white unto harvest; and He was sending us into those fields just as the Father had sent Him (John 4:34-38).

That means "missions" is simply an extension of His life, working through your life, to reach this generation with the love of God for a lost humanity. God is not asking us to give money to missions, but to make missions the central passion of our lives!

The church, as the corporate expression of the body of Christ, exists only to fulfill His will. And what is His will? He is "... not willing that any should perish, but that all should come to repentance." (2 Peter 3:9) Christ meant His church to be primarily a missionary organization—or better yet, a missionary organism.

The body of Christ, His church, is the living presence of a God whose heart is pounding with a passion for lost and dying souls. We must therefore be fellowshipping and worshipping with one thing in mind, reaching lost men and women wherever they are. We are to be a people willing to exchange anything and everything we have for the pearl of great price— the kingdom of God.

Is the Christ we worship and follow today the same Christ of the Gospels? Jesus was always pressing on to preach the Gospel in the next village. His heart's cry and prayer was for the dead and dying, for the lost, sick and undone. And the heart of every true disciple who follows in the steps of Jesus will be the same. We must be willing, as He was, to let everything go for the sake of lost souls—to give our lives to recapture just one lost inch of territory from darkness and hell. How can a church that does not reflect this spirit really be the bride of Christ?

What explanation or rationalization can we offer to explain the condition of Christianity today? The Bible offers us little help. It doesn't give much space to descriptions of a church which appears to be nothing less than a headless corpse.

How else can we describe a church body that appears to have fallen so far away from the commands of its mind—the Lord Jesus? Let me elaborate:

Feed Me First Fixation

We have a feed-me-first fixation. Christianity today is stuck in a rut of self-development. It is a me-and-mine style religion that survives on an endless diet of books, cassettes, conferences and seminars.

This fat-head faith has produced a generation of Christians who know all the answers but won't cross the street to help a neighbor in spiritual distress. This demonic reasoning goes, "Me first—after all, I can't help others until I help myself!"

We're content to sit in our comfortable pews week after week sucking on our spiritual baby bottles—as long as the religious entertainment offered doesn't interfere with lunch or the ball game.

That this style of religion has no effect whatsoever on our Monday morning lifestyle doesn't matter. It wasn't meant to make a difference at work, school or play in the first place. Our newest churches, with their air-conditioned atriums and gymnasiums, are being designed with the best ambiance money can buy. The designers don't want us to feel too much different there from the way we do at the mall or health club.

Our churches are patterning their architecture, evangelism and programs after the world, rather than the dictates of Christ through the Holy Spirit. For far too long, we've grabbed the latest fad in the world and baptized it into the church by adding a cute phrase or two. So "Jazzercise" became "Praisercise," and computer dating services became Christian singles' clubs. Rock 'n' roll emerged as " Christian rock music," and lately the heavy metal sound has been reborn as something called "Christian shock-rock." The list goes on and on. There are hundreds of examples.

A look at our church activity calendars reveals not a body of givers, but a society of receivers. Even our prayer meetings are little more than "bless-me" clubs. Could it be that we have let our churches become elaborate social programs with the name of God tacked on as an afterthought? Was Karl Marx right in this case? Isn't this kind of religion really a narcotic—"the opiate of the people"?

This is "convenience store" Christianity. The pastor's main job is to find ways to sugarcoat the Gospel message, making sure that he preaches a gospel that offends no one and runs a church that meets every imaginable mental and physical need.

It is a religion that loves to quote "charity begins at home" when the subject of missions comes up. It reminds us that Jerusalem must get in line to be fed first, but never gets around to quoting the part of the verse about "Judea and Samaria" and especially the "uttermost parts of the earth."

What does the Lord Jesus think of our religious merry-go-round?

The question that must be asked of every Christian activity we support is simply this: "Will this event create any impact on a lost and dying world?" If the answer is no then we must reconsider sponsoring it. We must ask if this is something from our agenda or His.

"But be ye doers of the word, and not hearers only." (James 1:22)

We have switched to a retreat and survival mode. Actually confronting the takeover of our school systems and institutions by decades of secular humanism is too much of a strain for our kind of religion. That would require going out and witnessing to the publicans and sinners of our day.

So we are running into temporary survival shelters such as Christian schools, religious radio and TV broadcasts, Christian concerts and a myriad of other escapisms.

The controlling force behind this massive retreat from the post-Christian, secularized culture of the West is fear rather than holiness. It is laziness rather than righteousness. And it is born from a lack of love rather than a genuine desire for separation. Could it be that these "good things" are really enemies of the best?

"For God hath not given us the spirit of fear; but of power, and of love, and of a sound mind." (2 Timothy 1:7)

Chapter 4

What Really Is Going On?

*W*e *have established a social caste system in our churches and institutions.* I thought only Hinduism had a system of social discrimination, but the American experience proves that religion by itself almost always divides rather than unites people. There are those who congregate in churches for all kinds of reasons other than the biblical one!

Many churches will sell out and move their property if a neighborhood starts to change racially or economically. No cost is too great to preserve the class distinctions that created the church in the first place. We will pay any price to maintain a church without people who are different from us in any way. Could it be that at the basis of most of our denominations and local church splits is not a pious struggle for truth—but an invisible system of discrimination against others based on age, race, education and economic background?

And what a tragedy we see on the mission fields when some of these same denominations try to export their schisms and divisive teachings to the churches of the Third World.

Let's face it. We like to be with our own kind. A church that asks us to love and reach out to the unlovely or to those different from us is unthinkable—yet it was the core of Christ's evangelistic lifestyle. We need to repent of the loveless, intolerant, self-centered Christianity that has become one of the most distinguishing characteristics of the church today.

Some modern church growth teachers are now openly applying Madison Avenue marketing techniques to further divide and create churches based on demographics rather than spiritual birth. This used to be done by tiny committees of racial bigots who met secretly. Today it is being taught as church growth in some of our seminaries!

"But if ye have respect to persons, ye commit sin, and are convinced of the law as transgressors." (James 2:9)

We are fascinated by having the best and the biggest. Social scientists say that the last sign of life in any movement comes when it starts to build monument-style buildings. Why do we insist on building the largest and most impressive structures in our city when people on the other side of town are hungry, jobless and worshipping in storefronts?

Why do we construct extravagant, oversized, inefficient buildings at all? What dark motive in us makes us want to be the biggest and the best? We need to be asking questions of this pattern since a typical new church in America now costs as much as 2,000 simple "prayer houses" would in the Third World. Who taught us that "bigger is better" and "nothing is too good for the house of the Lord?" Did God tell us this or have we learned it from the world?

How can we have some churches which are making monthly mortgage payments of $50,000 and still say they don't have enough in the budget for missions? Can we square this extravagance with the commands of our Lord who said, "How can ye believe, which receive honour one of another? ..." (John 5:44)

We are taken up with bumper-sticker theology. Any kind of spiritual thought that goes beyond "how to have a happy family" seems to be incomprehensible to modern Christians. The only kind of Christianity we want is a pragmatic kind that shows us how to have a positive mental attitude, get ahead with our career plans, win friends and influence people.

What's happened is that we've made over our theology and

preaching agenda into an image of ourselves. When I first began to preach about the necessity for a transformed and obedient life, someone would always come up to me and say, "Let's be careful here not to put people on guilt trips and teach legalism."

Such people want the Gospel and the Bible to stop with the phrase, "Christians aren't perfect, they're just forgiven." That's the end of their theology. That's all that fits on their bumper sticker!

Whatever Happened to the Teachings of Jesus?

Well, that's not the Gospel—and I'm not teaching perfectionism either. But we have to question a Christianity that has so distorted the doctrine of grace that a simple call to obedience is mistaken for legalism. Challenging people to live the normal Christian life rather than accommodate themselves to sin is not a guilt trip or manipulation. These phrases are frequently used today as a smoke-screen defense by self-serving believers who don't want their fantasy-land religion upset by the truth.

This narrow view of salvation has impoverished our faith more than we realize. Whatever happened to the teachings of Jesus on eternal judgment in hell? Why don't we warn people about the terrible punishment that awaits them if they don't turn back to God now? It's astonishing that so-called Bible-believing Christians have, in effect, taken a pair of scissors and snipped out vast sections of the Scriptures. Jesus lived daily with an awareness of the awful consequences of rejecting the grace of God—but why isn't His body connected today to the passion of a Savior who died to save men and women from eternal flames? How can we be casual about the lost world when God considered it so important that His only solution was Calvary?

"This people honoureth me with their lips, but their heart is far from me. Howbeit in vain do they worship me, teaching for doctrines the commandments of men." (Mark 7:6,7)

We have spoiled our children and youth. Why is it that the young people of our churches are given fun and games rather than the challenge of the Great Commission?

The preteen and teenage years are so critical. This is when most young people choose their careers and mates—probably the two biggest decisions which determine the course of any believer's life. Anyone who has ever worked with adolescents will tell you that this is probably the highest point in our lives for energy and idealism. Teens want to test out the ethics and morality of their church and parents to see if it really works.

Will Parents Back This Kind of Program?

But what are we giving them instead? The standard answer is to hire a youth director to plan parties and trips based around the premise: "You can be a Christian and have fun, too!" How many millions of our youth have been ruined by the introduction of this worldly Christianity just at the moment in life when they most need to see reality?

What would happen if instead we treated our youth with total seriousness, exposing them to mission field learning experiences? Opportunities to love and sacrifice for others? To serve on the front lines of the Gospel?

Will parents back this kind of program? If not, why not? How long can we go on ducking this question?

We have ruled out the supernatural and opted for self-sufficient, computerized Christianity. Technology is the modern-day magic of the West. It gives its users an incredible but false sense of power and control. To many today, knowledge and information have become equal to doing.

This is why the Western church has become the world's greatest collector of knowledge and expertise. And this is also why we're so dependent today on consultants. How many pastors spend far more time meeting with church-growth consultants, fund-raisers and salesmen than seeking the face of God for His will, plans and solutions?

We are becoming more and more dependent on *horizontal*, rationalistic, here-and-now solutions to our problems. We've become terrific consumers of products, seminars, shortcuts—anything, it seems, which does not require us to wait on the

Lord for *vertical* solutions to our dilemmas.

Stand outside a typical church next week and watch the congregation leave the worship service. Why do so many look as if they've just left the local movie theater, laughing and casual? Why are others sad and troubled with unsolved personal problems? Why are some so obviously bound by addictions and sin? Are these the faces of people who have had a face-to-face encounter with the living God? Where is the reverence and awe we would expect from a people who have just witnessed the miraculous? What is really going on in our churches today?

The haunting question that must be asked about the status of Christianity in the West is this: "Why do a people who have so much have so little? With all this knowledge and skill, why is there no great move of God in North America today?"

When are we going to look ourselves in the mirror and say, "OK, I know enough now. I've trained enough. I've consulted enough. What am I going to do about my knowledge of God and His ways? When is my life going to demonstrate His compassion to the needy world around me?"

We are following false shepherds. The church today is being ravaged by deceived men who spread half-gospels and lead millions of people astray with false teachings. I don't want to take time and space here to list examples of these religious con-artists, and there would be very little profit in doing so anyway. It's sufficient to say that they're everywhere, and many of them sound doctrinally correct.

But we should be asking some even more relevant questions, not resting until we get their answers in our spirits: "Why do we let these people into our homes via radio and television? Why do we go to their seminars, conferences and churches? Why do we buy their books and tapes? Why do we give millions of dollars to keep their flimsy ministries going?"

Few Christians can say they haven't been taken in by these wolves at one time or another. What is it, then, that is making us so vulnerable to their seductive doctrines?

"But there were false prophets also among the people, even as there shall be false teachers among you, who privily shall bring in damnable heresies, even denying the Lord that bought them, ... beguiling unstable souls: an heart they have exercised with covetous practices; ... These are wells without water, clouds that are carried with a tempest: to whom the mist of darkness is reserved for ever." (2 Peter 2:1,14,17)

Hyperactivism and Dead Works

We have fallen victim to hyperactivism and dead works. Modern churches are among the most frenzied organizations in the world. In almost any average-sized community, the calendar is so full that you can keep going almost day and night on a year-round basis. The unwary believer is challenged constantly to join this merry-go-round of religious activities and fellowship.

Because yielding the time and money we control to Christ is such an important test of stewardship, many a sincere but naive Christian falls into this trap of carnal activism. For many, workaholism is as addictive as alcohol or smoking. Such victims of religious "busy-ness" are little different from cultists on the treadmill of earning their salvation by penance, selling books or doing good works.

Their bookshelves are full of Christian books and tapes. Some even give up network television entirely. They're always off to another meeting or seminar. Christian broadcasts and tapes play in their cars. They're the kind of people who are present every time the church door opens.

But in the wake of these busy Christians are often broken homes, relationships and churches. Family, friends and co-workers shake their heads and instinctively pull back. Jesus predicted that the branch connected to the vine would produce much spiritual fruit. But too often our frantic lives are barren.

Where in our oh, so busy, busy lives of Christian service is Christ Himself? Where is the fruit that would authenticate our works? Are we merely acting out the motions of the Christian life or is the Spirit of God being released in our religious activities?

To answer this question and so many others, we need to cross a bridge. Too few modern Christians even know it exists—but there is no other way for the world-weary believer to go. It means giving up our fairy-tale notions about Christ and Christianity. It means stepping away from the comfortable Christianity—the one we have conformed to our culture. But for the man and woman God uses, there can be no other direction. There is no exit but the road to reality.

In the next chapter, I'll show you how you can take your first step on the path to authentic Christianity.

Chapter 5

How Long Will We Be Duped?

By now I'm sure you're already asking yourself the most critical of all questions: *Is there any hope for a people who have fallen so far away from authentic Christian living?*

Recently a dear friend and fellow minister in New York City went through an experience that has to be every parent's worst nightmare. And I need to tell this story at this point because I think it parallels vividly what I've been trying to say about Christians and Christian culture in the West today. This true story gives me hope and confidence in the measureless grace of God. It gives me faith to keep believing for a great revival in the West.

For the sake of those involved, I'll call their daughter Mary. Although Mary appeared to be a model child in her early years, she and the whole family obviously had many unresolved spiritual and mental problems. Mary grew up in the church, surrounded with every physical and spiritual advantage a child could have. I had stayed in their home on several occasions—yet nothing prepared me for the shock of what this beautiful girl became in her rebellious teenage years.

As a high school sophomore, she began having behavior problems at church and school. Frustrated family and friends couldn't get through to her. Numerous attempts at counseling only made the problems worse. Mary refused to listen to even the most loving advice. It seemed that if something was against the rules, Mary had to do it—the more outrageous, the better!

Eventually, no one could control her. She began disappearing for days on end to act out a prodigal life of drug abuse and illicit sex that led to suicide attempts. Her father and other friends from church often walked the streets of Times Square looking for her among the thousands of teenage runaways who were then attracted there from all over the nation. After many attempts to stop her, one discouraged friend after another quit trying to get through.

Thus began two years of life in and out of jails, institutions and hospitals. Mary's life was still on a fast track to destruction when the Lord finally reached her in a rescue mission. Thank God, her story has a happy ending. She turned back to Christ, and today is living for the Lord.

But I tell this story of Mary the prodigal because it could easily be the story of the Christian church in America today.

We also are prodigal. As congregations—and as individuals—we're out of touch with reality. Like Mary, we're not listening, not submitting to our spiritual head. What's more, we're in such total rebellion against Christ that we're hardly aware anything is wrong!

In our story, Mary finally came to that point where she realized she had to return to God or end up dead in some back alley. But although Christianity in the West today is desperately sick, still we refuse to admit our need for crisis intervention. We're so busy with our own plans, agendas, activities and pleasures that we've lost sight of the one and only purpose for which Christ redeemed us.

The World Is Dictating Its Standards to Us

The situation is grave. How long can a loving God continue to let us go on without chastisement and judgment? Individually and collectively, we are like children captured by forces we cannot control or understand. The world is dictating its standards to us, and believers have been taken captive by the powers of darkness.

We are living in a generation that is no more the body of Christ exercising authority over the powers of this world. Instead, the world is dictating its sordid standards to us.

We are not manifesting the life and power of Christ. Instead, we're living in captivity and bondage.

We are not storming the gates of hell. Instead, we're falling over one another in retreat—looking for fox holes, hiding from the enemy.

Why is the army of God in retreat before the world, the flesh and the devil? Will we ever again be able to display the glorious love of the living Christ? Will this dark and dying world ever see Jesus in us again?

My answer is yes—a thousand times, yes!

There is a way out of this mess. We don't have to remain living in powerless, insipid hypocrisy. God has ordained for us to demonstrate Christ to a lost and dying world. He wills for us to have victory. He wants us to recover our lost authority and live again as He did.

Authentic Christianity is not reserved only for missionary heroes and super-saints. It is not something that happens only on faraway foreign fields or in the pages of the Bible. It must and will blossom forth right on the street where you live, at your work, in your school. It is for every believer, whatever your calling or circumstances. Jesus wants to extend Himself into your world. However, for this miracle of abundant life to happen, you must make daily choices. God will never force you to walk the road to spiritual reality. It is a journey you must decide to begin personally.

We Must See the Real Jesus

Spiritual reality begins when, like Moses at the burning bush, we come face to face with the living God. Up until that moment, Moses had tried in his own power to deliver Israel without success. His self-appointed rescue attempts floundered, but then for the first time, he saw the invisible Creator on the mount of God. What a transformation came to this disgraced prince. Moses was empowered from on high. From then on, he counted it a privilege to forsake the splendor of Egypt and suffer with the people of God.

Could it be that many of us have not yet turned aside at the burning bush to gaze at the real Jesus? We must begin our spiritual journey there—not with the plastic substitutes so often offered on the air waves today. How long will we go on being duped by the phony "christs" that are circulated by the purveyors of TV's pop religion?

The secret of the abundant life is Christ and Christ alone. We must see the real Jesus. We must have a correct vision of who He is, and therefore who we are to incarnate and serve during our time on planet Earth. Only then will we begin to rediscover the authority, glory and power of His majesty.

One of the most revealing images of the real Jesus is found in Colossians 1:13-20. Here we find Him to be the Lord of all things visible and invisible ... thrones, dominions, rulers and authorities ... by and for whom all things were created, and for whom all things consist ... the firstborn from the dead, that in all things He might have preeminence ... the one in whom it pleased the Father that all fullness should dwell.

What a mighty God we serve! The whole universe, everything that we can see and cannot see, was created for Him. He is head of the church and our Lord. We were made for Him and His pleasure.

This is not the same God we are being taught to manipulate and order about by the superstars of American religion. The true Jesus *rules*—and that means He rules us. The true Jesus *reigns*—and that means He reigns over us. We must learn that our proper place is at the feet of the Lord Jesus. Only then will we find the key to unlock His plans and purposes in our individual lives.

What awe, reverence and worship the very names of our Lord should evoke in the spirit of every true believer. *And thou shalt call his name ... Jesus, Prince of Peace, Mighty God, Wonderful, Counselor, Holy One, Lamb of God, Prince of Life, Lord God Almighty, Lion of the Tribe of Judah, Root of David, Word of Life, Author and Finisher of Our Faith, Advocate, The Way, Dayspring, Lord of All, I Am, Son of God, Shepherd and Bishop of Souls, Messiah, The Truth, Savior, Chief Cornerstone, King of Kings, Righteous Judge, Light of the World, Head of the Church, Morning Star, Sun of Righteousness, Lord Jesus Christ, Chief Shepherd, Resurrection and Life, Horn of Salvation, Governor, The Alpha and Omega.*

Though He humbled Himself to come as a human baby, revealed Himself as a servant and died as a criminal—this Jesus is the same yesterday, today and forever. Though He is Jehovah Jirah, our provider, He is not the Santa Claus so many have made Him out to be. As we have a fuller realization of our true place in creation, the wonder of Christ dwelling in us becomes the beginning of understanding. Yet this awareness remains a secret to so many in our age, because our real worship has shifted from the King of the universe. We adore our own abilities, bodies, minds and talents rather than the God who gave them to us.

Chapter 6

God's Purpose for You

Contrary to the popular thinking of Christianity today, the Lord did not reach down and save us from sin and death so that we might be merely happy, healthy and wealthy. Those who teach this have invented another gospel and portray a false christ—the god of this age rather than the God of the Bible. A gospel without the cross is no Gospel at all.

God's purpose for man, from the moment He created us, has never changed. We have always been destined for the throne—created to rule with the one who created all things for Himself.

First, we are to be the body—the hands and feet of Jesus in this present world.

"And he is the head of the body, the church," says Colossians 1:18. All who believe and have been baptized into Christ are the church. Now we know that our head, Jesus Christ, is at the right hand of the Father making intercession for us. But the Bible says His body is somewhere else. His body is us. We are left here on earth to carry out His desires and will.

The purpose of the body is to fulfill the commands, desires and wishes of the head. We are attached to the head so that we might manifest the mind of Christ and do His will on earth.

God has so ordered the world that right now we are His primary agents of redemption to lost humanity. Our hands are His hands, our feet are His feet, our tongues are His tongue. This means that the basic way God expresses His limitless love today is through the church. Lost men and women in this dark and dying world will not be found unless we search for them.

In 1 John 4:17 we read, "As he is, so are we in this world." I love the way Moffatt translates this in his classic version of the English New Testament. It reads, "... since in this world we are living as He is." This makes it abundantly clear that a believer's life ought to so represent Christ that the world can once again see Jesus. We follow Him in a way that others can taste again the presence of Jesus walking and living among them.

The only way that Christ is presently incarnated to a lost world is through us—we are carrying on and extending His presence, His Word and His works to a new generation. When Jesus walked the shores of Galilee, He revealed the image of the Father to lost and sinful men. This glorious ministry is now ours as we reveal the mind of Christ to the lost around us.

Second, we are ambassadors of Christ in the courts of a rebellious world.

As Jesus prepared to leave this world and return to His Father, He called the disciples together. "All authority is given to Me in heaven and in earth," He declared. "Now go in My name— as the Father has sent Me, so I send you." Later, under the inspiration of the Holy Spirit, Paul described us as "Christ's ambassadors."

An ambassador is a person who represents his country in an alien land. He is given authority by his government to represent the best interests of his nation. He can make and break contracts for his government and handle all kinds of affairs, both civil and military. Ambassadors exercise enormous power and influence, particularly when they represent a powerful kingdom.

Our Citizenship Is in Heaven

The Bible tells us that we are no more citizens of this world. Our citizenship is in heaven. We have been translated from the kingdom of darkness to the kingdom of light. We belong to our sovereign King and His name is Jesus, King of kings and Lord of lords.

As ambassadors sent to this world from another kingdom, how then are we to live and represent our King?

Under a real monarchy, you do not debate the wishes of the king. You simply obey without discussion or question. The Lord Jesus left us with a clear picture of His desires for our generation. We know from Scripture exactly what He wants us to be doing. We even know what kind of behavior He wants the world to see in us, because He taught us His lifestyle both by word and example.

Third, He wants us to operate in His authority and power.

Christ wants us to move in the same mysterious authority and power that surrounded His earthly ministry. In Matthew 7:29 and many other places we read, "For he taught them as one having authority, and not as the scribes." He confounded the best academics and theologians of His day—as well as kings and rulers of all sorts.

From the beginning of the church, we see this same quality reproduced among the apostles. In Acts 4, Peter and John are dragged before the Sanhedrin—the most powerful religious court in Israel. They are questioned about where they received authority and power to heal a cripple.

In verse 10 Peter, in the power of the Holy Spirit, boldly replies, "Be it known unto you all, and to all the people of Israel, that by the name of Jesus Christ of Nazareth, whom ye crucified, whom God raised from the dead, even by him doth this man stand here before you whole."

This was an eloquent answer, and it stunned the lawyers and priests. In verse 13 we read, "Now when they saw the boldness of Peter and John, and perceived that they were unlearned and ignorant men, they marvelled; and they took knowledge of them, that they had been with Jesus."

Now we get the full picture. These highly educated, suave, sophisticated leaders recognized that something unusual was happening. Something out of this world was going on! They weren't used to having a bunch of blue-collar "rednecks" answer like that.

Even Unbelievers Recognize the Power of Jesus

By this they knew that these less-educated fishermen had been with Jesus. The same energy that blazed out at them from the Galilean they had killed was alive again in these disciples. Those who did not want such light and life were very threatened.

So we see that through Christ we are potentially restored to live as God originally intended man to live in the garden of Eden. God gave man authority in Genesis chapter one—and now we are expected to live and serve Him in that power.

Does this "job description" make you feel a little uncomfortable? I did, too, when I compared the lives we lead today with the life of a normal Christian as described in the New Testament. How is it possible to live as His body, be His ambassador, operate in His power and authority? Isn't God making impossible demands on His fallen creation?

Of course not! God would not ask us to have this kind of authority and power-filled life without also making a provision for us to live such a supernatural existence.

The key scripture that explains the secret of this divine indwelling is Galatians 2:20. "I am crucified with Christ: nevertheless I live; yet not I, but Christ liveth in me: and the life which I now live in the flesh I live by the faith of the Son of God, who loved me, and gave himself for me." God does not commit His authority at random to anyone. This verse is basic to understanding the process of incarnating Christ to our generation.

Christ's life is mine by faith. It is called by many names, but this exchanged life is the only acceptable New Testament norm. Anything less is a sick substitute for reality.

I have been crucified—it is no longer I who live. Our ego is dead. Our will is submitted and surrendered. We cannot let circumstances, family, friends, the government, the media, religious leaders or Satan himself lead us to anything less than reality.

The Lost Message of the Cross

But something is still very wrong.

Why are so few living out the "not I, but Christ" lifestyle that Paul describes in Galatians 2:20? Although God eagerly desires to manifest Himself within us, I believe it is because so few of us have learned to let the cross do its deadly work in our flesh on a daily basis. We haven't yet come to a full understanding of the cross.

We must return to Calvary. The glory and presence of Christ will return to our lives and churches only when we have rediscovered the cross of Christ.

The cross has two operations. First, on it Christ paid the penalty for our sins, and thus bought our eternal salvation. But it doesn't stop there. The second work of the cross provides for our ongoing sanctification—the daily, continuous crucifixion of our flesh. This great doctrine is not very popular lately because it requires a voluntary acceptance of death to ego or self.

Someone has put it this way, "If self is on the throne, then Christ is on the cross. If Christ is on the throne, then self is on the cross."

This is why Paul says in 2 Corinthians 4:10 that we are "always bearing about in the body the dying of the Lord Jesus, that the life also of Jesus might be made manifest in our body." Accepting death to my ego is the only way to manifest the life of Christ. Putting my "self" to death is the only way to exchange my life for His.

I believe that this is the real meaning of Galatians 2:20 where Paul says, "I am crucified with Christ."

So here is the spiritual law of the flesh: *The measure to which I will manifest the life of Christ is the same measure to which I am willing to put my "self" to death.*

When Jesus walked on earth, God was showing us not only what He was like but also what He wanted man to be like. Jesus had authority and power because He constantly submitted Himself to the will of the Father in every matter. Christ pleased the Father and reflected the Father perfectly because He perfectly put to death His flesh. And we repeat this cycle as we submit to our head, the Lord Jesus.

This is the life that is connected to Jesus, the head, on a decision-by-decision basis. It is the submitted, dead-to-self life that the Lord can animate and use for His glory. It is the only kind of life He will empower and use.

If we're rightly connected to the head in this way, it would be hard to imagine making any decision without first submitting it to Christ for His approval. What would that do to the way we spend our time? What does Christ say about the TV and the films we view, the music we listen to, or the catalogs and magazines we read?

What about our activities—church, clubs, leisure time, friendships, hobbies, prayer, service, sports and study?

What about our relationships with boyfriends, girlfriends, mentors and role models? Whom do we idolize and pattern our lives after?

What about our purchases, both the large and small ones? Is our shopping basket under His control? Does He direct the checks we write? What about the "big buys"—our car, home and insurance?

What about our intake of food and drink? Is Christ or our appetites in control?

And of course, there are those major decisions in life—full-time missionary service, career and job plans, education and the choice of a mate.

For the Christian, none of these things is any longer a personal decision. It is not what others say, what self says or what circumstances dictate. The only valid question is always, What does Christ say to me about this decision?

But most of us find ourselves making even the big decisions without prayer and waiting for guidance from the Holy Spirit.

Obviously, the gap between this kind of biblical Christianity and the shallow spirituality of our day is a significant one. How different is this kind of self-sacrificing faith from the pleasure-seeking, self-serving, wimpy religion so often preached and practiced in our churches!

Chapter 7

A Lifelong Battle

How the flesh twists and turns to refuse the work of the cross! Our conversion to Christ begins a lifelong battle with the flesh—it is not removed once and for all. The Bible tells us that the flesh lusts against the Spirit.

When we are born again, our old nature doesn't disappear. Instead, a new nature is introduced, and the struggle begins. The two of them battle to the death daily.

The old nature cries out "me!," "mine!" and "ours!"; while the new nature is replying "His!," "others!" and "theirs!"

How can we respond successfully to the attacks of the flesh? Here are several important defenses:

First, don't seek mystical spiritual experiences to defeat the flesh.

I have counseled with hundreds of believers who struggle daily with all kinds of fleshly problems—jealousy, lustful desires, selfishness, hate, backbiting and the others listed in Galatians and Corinthians. Many are looking for a shortcut to victory in some mystical experience.

Why do we love to collect certain spiritual experiences and boast in them? When you come to the West as a visitor, almost everyone you meet looks for a label. They want to know if you're "fundamental" or "Spirit-filled."

However, I've noticed that virtually no one asks if you're

dead to the flesh. This is one experience that's not high on our lists.

But the fact is that until we've learned to go to the cross and speak death to our ego-drives that lust against the Spirit, there can be no reality in the Christian life. No obedience and victory occur without the cross.

In one meeting where I gave this message, a young lady came up to me after the meeting and asked me to lay hands on her and pray for a need she had. I asked her what the problem was.

She said to me, "Brother K.P., I have this terrible smoking problem and I'm sure it's a demon. If you pray for me, I believe I can be delivered."

As I talked further with her, I realized that she was an individual who really didn't take her faith seriously. She was looking for a shortcut, an easy experience rather than to come face to face with dying to the flesh. She was eager to blame demons and others, but the problem was her own will.

No Shortcut

The Bible contains unchanging laws. Therefore, we cannot cast out, bind with spiritual words, deny or command away that which the Bible declares needs to be crucified—our flesh.

There is no shortcut to the victorious life. God is not going to put your flesh to death for you. He did His part on Calvary. Now we are told in Romans 8 to "mortify the deeds of the body." We must choose to experience the reality of Galatians 2:20.

Some people believe they need to wait on God to deliver them, to come and crucify their flesh. They have a false notion that they have to remain neutral and let God do some kind of "sanctification work" on their flesh.

Nothing could be farther from the truth. His work was completed on the cross nearly 2,000 years ago. Now we have to act on the freedom He has earned for us. We are called upon to put the flesh to death on a moment-by-moment basis—by faith—in the same way that we receive salvation in the first place. *It is all of grace by faith.* The only human action required is the submission of your will to His.

Second, lay aside religious pride regarding your knowledge, traditions and denominational identity.

Obviously, the gap between biblical Christianity and the way we live today is a very big one. One of the most common stumbling blocks to victory is pride in our religious doctrines, denominations and traditions.

You can brag that you belong to the true church all you want to, but it makes no difference. Whether you're fundamental, evangelical, Spirit-filled or whatever, it doesn't change the fact that the Bible says clearly, "If you live after the flesh, you shall surely die."

Of course, the devil comes along and says surely you'll not die—just as he lied to Eve in the garden. But the truth is that if you continue to listen to your favorite teachers—living outwardly the way your little group says to, but living inwardly after the flesh—you will still die.

At the judgment, the Lord will not ask about your fundamentalist beliefs, if your church can trace its roots back to the apostles, or the manner in which you were baptized.

The only thing that will matter then is the words of Romans 8:13,14: "For if ye live after the flesh, ye shall die: but if ye through the Spirit do mortify the deeds of the body, ye shall live. For as many as are led by the Spirit of God, they are the sons of God."

The test of our spiritual reality hinges on how we have handled the flesh, not on our creeds or anything else of this world, including other "pride of life" sins such as education, birth, parentage, social class or race.

Even after 20 years of preaching, Paul said in 1 Corinthians 9:27 that he buffeted his body to bring it under submission. Why? He was afraid that after preaching to everybody else, he might be disqualified.

The Truth Will Make Us Free

Paul knew that right doctrine without right living is worthless in the sight of God. We seem to forget that the Pharisees of Jesus' day were correct in their doctrine. They were outwardly righteous in their lives. They kept the law far better than we do today. These were respected clergy. They knew the truth and were superactive in church—but they still went ahead and killed the King of glory. We must stop trusting in our religious beliefs and labels. If we really know the truth, then the truth will make us free—and that means free from self and dead to the flesh.

Third, we must give up all hope that somehow we can reform and redeem the flesh.

In Romans 7:18, Paul says, "For I know that in me (that is, in my flesh,) dwelleth no good thing. ..." We don't want to admit that today. We still want to display our degrees, experience, insights and talents. We have fallen in love with our knowledge, management skills and technology. We have taken our eyes off the Giver and focused them on the gifts.

Unless we as humans are tied into and connected to Christ our head, we are nothing and have no purpose. Even the greatest geniuses of art and science are only a marred, shallow reflection of the God who created our universe in the first place. Jesus died that we might be plugged into Him, as the branches are part of the vine. Living off our own resources, not attached to the vine, leads only to dryness, death and flames.

The Bible tells us that all the works of the flesh will be burned up. How hard it is to accept this. We still want to do the work of the Lord in our own power and strength—be it with our education, talent or wealth. But in the eyes of God, it is still just educated flesh, talented flesh or rich flesh—all to be burned up in judgment and rejected by Him.

We must come to that place of absolute understanding that as human beings there is nothing in us—not our looks, background, education, riches, talents or anything else you can add—which will enable us to live the kind of life God wants us to live in our generation.

We find Paul in Philippians 3:4-12, writing from a prison cell, yet still crying out and longing to experience a little more death to self. Just as his Master set His face to the cross, Paul was determined to continue to say no to the flesh and yes to the Spirit until the end of his life.

"For we are the circumcision," he says, "which worship God in the spirit, and rejoice in Christ Jesus, and have no confidence in the flesh." (Philippians 3:3)

In this passage, Paul lists many of the beautiful talents, experiences, gifts and knowledge which he possessed—and then he says he counts them as manure. He said, "I start from zero."

The idea is never to reform the flesh, sanctify the flesh or cleanse it—the victory formula is always the same: "Put it to death."

The concept of being "conformed to his death" needs to be seen for what it is, *an ongoing process*. We may be nobodies in the eyes of the world, but if we are partaking of His death, then the glory and power of Christ will surely be manifested. This is why the disenfranchised, the humble and the poor are so often selected by God as objects of His grace. In God's economy, the cross always comes before Pentecost. Death always comes before life.

What Does My Master Want?

The Spirit-controlled Christian will apply this principle throughout each day, praying that each action and decision will be according to the will of Christ rather than the flesh.

To those that wanted to follow Him, Jesus said, "If any man will come after me, let him deny himself, and take up his cross, and follow me." (Matthew 16:24) Jesus invites us to take up the weapon of our execution if we want to follow Him.

In another place He said, "If you cannot love Me more than father, mother, son, daughter—*even your own life*—you cannot be My disciple" (see Luke 14:26).

You see, following Christ means making a 180-degree turnaround. It is an exchange. My life for His life. There is no longer any parallel existence of both together.

It is no longer what I want. It is not my will, my way, my plans, my wishes—but only what He wants. The question is always, What does my Master say? What does He want?

Then all that I have is His. My hands, legs, heart, eyes, ears, finances, family, dreams and visions—everything belongs to Christ. He is able to live, breathe, walk, touch, weep, look and hear through the earthen vessel of my body.

The Lord Jesus Christ defeated Satan, not when He performed miracles and raised the dead, but when He went to the cross. As we are willing to choose the cross daily in our lives, we too will experience victory over sin, the world, the flesh and the devil.

Before we move on to the next chapters, which teach some of the practical lessons, it is important that you have consciously chosen death to self. If you're hungry for reality and want to go on with God, please stop right now and pray this prayer of surrender. Be sure to list specific areas of your life which you have not yet nailed to the cross.

> Lord Jesus, I confess that I have failed to yield
> to Your Spirit and submitted instead to my flesh
> in the matter of _____.
> Beginning this moment, show me Your will as
> I, by faith, put to death my flesh in this area
> through Your finished work on the cross.
> Amen.

If you will choose to pray this prayer sincerely in every decision area of your life, you will take the first step toward reality in your Christian life. This is the first bridge on the road to reality, and once it is crossed, you can begin to yield in other more specific areas of your daily life.

Part II

REDISCOVERING JESUS CHRIST

We can become images
of the Lord in our world today
as we cross new bridges
on our road to reality.

Chapter 8

No Pain, No Gain

We want it all—and we want it now. As a culture, the West is enslaved by a near worship of comfort and convenience. God taught me this lesson early in my American ministry. It has helped me to understand why the church has so often become a stumbling block to the Gospel, when it should be the powerhouse of missions in the world today.

It became clear to me when the Lord opened the door to preach in a small Southern church. During the morning service, the Holy Spirit moved mightily over the congregation. There was a great conviction about the lost millions of Asia.

The pastor was especially touched. With tears in his eyes, he stood before his people and confessed that his heart had been cold toward missions. But he said that the Lord had given him a new vision that morning and he wanted to see the congregation get involved in fulfilling the Great Commission.

He urged his people to pray about the needs of Asia and to return that evening to see our missionary slides. Again that night the Lord moved supernaturally, and many made decisions to adopt native missionaries.

It was early in our ministry, and in those days I often stayed overnight as a guest of the local pastor. After the meeting, he talked again about how the Lord had moved him.

At the time, we were planning a vision tour for pastors to come and see the work of native missionaries with their own eyes. So because of his intense interest, I offered this pastor an opportunity to join us for the tour.

He seemed fascinated as I told him how leaders like David Mains from The Chapel of the Air and many others had their ministries revolutionized by a visit to the field.

Then he asked questions, but not the ones I expected. He wanted to know about the 100-degree heat we would be experiencing in north India, how we would travel, what the food would be like and where we would be staying.

Finally, he turned to me and said something that was to become a revelation to me. "Brother K.P., I'm just a country boy. I've been raised on biscuits and gravy. I'd probably get diarrhea if I went, and besides I always ride in air-conditioned cars."

Sadly, he never visited the mission field, though I left the door open for him. Like millions, just the thought of some temporary discomfort was enough to keep him from the spiritual adventure of a lifetime.

Businesses, politicians and even many church leaders cater to this soft and rotten spot in the soul of our nation. Fortunes have been made by corporations that will provide services without lines and hassles, who have learned to satisfy the demands of the consumer with instant gratification.

But there is a dark and deadly side to this fascination with comfort and convenience. Every 20 seconds, somewhere in the United States, the life of an unborn child is snuffed out through abortion. The reason usually given? "We're just not ready to have a baby now." *Translated into plain English, this means that having the baby would be too inconvenient.*

If a new human life should happen to get in the way of our career and income goals, school schedules or marriage plans, the American solution of first choice is ruthless and simple: kill it. Nothing is allowed to get in the way of feeling good.

Abortion is one of the most shocking, yet entirely logical, extensions of this obsession with comfort, convenience and luxury. Less dramatic, but just as deadly to millions of lost souls in our world, is our unwillingness to make even small sacrifices to reach them.

Paying the Price of Pain

Where are believers who will make a deliberate calculation to accept sacrifice and suffering for the sake of following Christ? We'll never enter the enemy camp and storm the gates of hell until we realize again that a soldier does not live on feelings. Casualties, discomfort and injury are part of the program for victory. Real Christians accept suffering as a normal part of following Christ, just as mothers accept labor as a normal part of delivering a baby.

"No pain, no gain" applies to world evangelism as well as exercise programs! Until we can accept suffering, sacrifice and self-denial as routine and normal we will never see the Great Commission fulfilled in our generation.

But the distorted Madison Avenue ideals of the good life are deeply ingrained in our minds and lifestyles. They will not go without a conscious decision to become a servant rather than be served. Unless we choose the way of the cross, we will always find ourselves automatically falling into that pattern of extravagance and waste that has become the norm of this culture.

The visitor here is stunned at the way we live in a world of throwaway products. Bottles, cans, cups, towels and plates are thoughtlessly trashed here that would be treasured anywhere else in the world. Why won't we take the time to wash and reuse them? The reason is simple: convenience is king, and the average person wouldn't consider having it any other way.

Feeling Good Is Good Enough for Me

And we have imitated this "throwaway" lifestyle with our current practice of Christianity. Today we have substituted a religion of good vibes and trouble-free living for the commands of the Master. He said, "Take up your cross and follow Me," but we have clenched our fists and refused to open our palms. We won't receive the nail, because it would mean death to our "self." We demand instead to pleasure our desires for self-gratification. And we have found shepherds and Bible teachers who will give us a "feel good" theology to match and justify our lives of sinful rebellion.

The lyrics to a popular hit have become the national anthem of our current generation. The refrain goes, "Feeling good is good enough for me." How many millions live today with this as their guiding philosophy, including countless Christians?

Much of this popular "Santa Claus" religion today is centered around a horrible distortion of Bible doctrine and history. It is a teaching contrary to the central thrust of Scripture. It denies the demands of the Gospel and says, "You can have the good life now—and heaven besides!"

It tickles our ears to hear this religion taught. It promises us the services of a god who exists to solve all our problems— making us happy, healthy, popular, successful and rich. But this isn't the Jesus Christ that Paul and the apostles followed. Nor is it the God of Abraham, Moses, David or Elijah. It sounds much more like the false promises of Baal or the idol gods of paganism.

Christ's Call to Suffering

Jesus never apologized for calling His disciples to a life of self-denial. It is interesting to see the way He handled this teaching with those who offered to follow Him.

He promised homelessness. We read in Luke 9:57 of an individual who bragged that he would follow Jesus wherever He would go. But apparently he turned back when Jesus replied, "Foxes have holes, and birds of the air have nests; but the Son of man hath not where to lay his head." (Luke 9:58)

He promised broken relationships. Another man said he would go but needed to bury his father first. Jesus replied, "Let the dead bury their dead: but go thou and preach the kingdom of God." (Luke 9:60)

He promised separation and loneliness. A third would-be disciple said, "Lord, I will follow thee; but let me first go bid them farewell, which are at home at my house." Jesus replied, "No man, having put his hand to the plough, and looking back, is fit for the kingdom of God." (Luke 9:62)

It is obvious that Jesus will have no one among His followers who is wanting to put comfort, family ties or security in this world ahead of His kingdom. Jesus is saying, in effect, "I offer you what I have—hardship, hunger, labor, loneliness, rejection, sweat, tears and death. I'm a stranger and pilgrim in this world, and if you follow Me you'll have to break away from the clinging attachments of this present life."

The Gospels give another example. A rich young ruler wanted to follow Jesus and asked what he would have to do to inherit the kingdom. Jesus replied simply, "Go, sell all that you have and give it to the poor." The young man walked away sad.

Jesus obviously loved him. It must have hurt to see the young man go. But in this case and in all the other similar stories, you never once see Jesus going after these would-be disciples. There is no effort to pacify them or modify and soften the uncompromising demands of the cross. It is either "give up everything and follow Me" or "don't come at all."

To all those who would follow Him, He gave the same basic message. Those who save their lives will lose them—those who lose their lives for His sake will find them. The first shall be last and the last first.

There is no place in His band for those who are not willing to accept inconvenience, sufferings and uncertainty. This is still the price of following Christ today just as it was then.

I'm convinced the main reason why we are not impacting our generation for Christ is our refusal to be honest about Christianity. We have offered the world a gospel without sacrifice and suffering. We've done everything we can to apologize for Christ's demands and explain them away. We've told people that Jesus didn't really mean what He said—that they can have Christ without His cross.

The result is all around us. We have apologetic, defensive, shallow Christians whose faith can't turn the next corner, let alone turn the world upside down. Although we have millions of books and more head-knowledge than any generation in Christian history, we still stand powerless and defeated.

Chapter 9

Real Faith Doesn't Come Cheap

Throughout the Bible, you will find that those who followed God often paid with their lives:

In the very beginning, Abel was slain by his jealous brother after he pleased God with a blood sacrifice.

Noah was mocked and ridiculed for 120 years as a result of his obedience.

Abraham—the father of our faith—sought to serve God and paid a great price. It cost him everything. Not only did he leave father, mother, home and riches, but he didn't even know where he was going. He gave up his rights to the best pasture land when he let Lot choose the well-watered plains of Sodom. But the Lord had promised him that He would be his reward and that was enough for Abraham. He wanted God more than anything this world had to offer.

Later, God fulfilled His promise and gave Abraham a son, but then He came back and asked him to give up the boy. If God had asked for 50,000 sheep or 10,000 rams—anything Abraham had—it would have been given without question. But this really hurt. God was asking for everything, and still Abraham held nothing back.

Moses was another. He had the whole kingdom of Egypt in his hand. He was a prince, but he threw it all away. He refused to be called the son of Pharaoh's daughter and chose instead to suffer affliction with the people of God. The Bible says he walked away from it all because he saw Him who is invisible. He chose to suffer in order to fulfill God's plan for his life.

When you get to the judges and prophets, you find men of tears, sorrow, hurt and pain. They were beaten, stoned, killed and placed in dungeons. Hebrews 11 sums up the stories of dozens who paid for faith with life itself.

All but one of the New Testament apostles were martyred. They walked in the steps of the Master to a death like His, on their own crosses. Others were beheaded. Jesus said that a servant was not above his master.

In light of all this, I ask a simple question: "When did God change His plan and offer an easier method to live for Him?" Are modern evangelicals the only Christians in history to experience the power of the living God without paying a personal price?

No, I believe that God's ways are still the same. There is still a cross for each of us. There is still a path of suffering and sacrifice for every Christian who wants to manifest Christ.

Not Asceticism or Masochism

Please don't misunderstand me. I am not promoting asceticism or the self-infliction of wounds. There are still flagellants in the Philippines and many other countries who practice this heresy today, but that is not the mystery of suffering the Bible teaches.

True Christian suffering comes because we live for God and are serving the expansion of His kingdom. It is a positive sacrifice for the good of others. It is not a morbid, introspective act that one does to oneself to feel or become spiritual.

No, I'm saying that if you really mean to follow Christ, you will not be at peace until the whole world knows of Him. You will pay any price to see others know the love of God.

"Yea, and all that will live godly in Christ Jesus shall suffer persecution," says 2 Timothy 3:12. This is the meaning of suffering for Christ. It is true in all countries and at all times. How dare we think that we have a right to be an exception?

In the book of Acts, we find Paul going to Jerusalem despite the fact that he knew afflictions, beatings, imprisonment and sorrow lay ahead. He was warned. He didn't have to go, but he chose to love the Lord more than his own life.

Paul took a calculated risk. He said, "Neither count I my life dear unto myself, so that I might finish my course with joy, and the ministry, which I have received of the Lord Jesus, to testify the gospel of the grace of God." (Acts 20:24)

This is a perfect example of the proper attitude toward suffering. It is never something we desire for its own sake, but something that we choose because it is necessary for the sake of the Gospel.

Suffering Authenticates Our Faith and Calling

When Paul's apostleship was challenged, he used a defense in 2 Corinthians that mocks our current "convenience store" Christianity. He does not rest his case on the testimony of his call, conversion, birth or background—as wonderful as all these were. He barely mentions his incredible spiritual gifts. There is almost no reference to his accreditation, educational degrees, ordination or memberships. He does not point to material blessings such as buildings, vestments or wealth because he had given these all up to follow in the steps of Jesus. In short, he relied on none of the criteria that we would look toward today.

Instead, he uses his suffering and sacrifice as the basis of his defense. Paul is saying that trials and tribulations authenticate, verify and vindicate his ministry. To Paul, suffering is the proof of his discipleship—not recognition or the symbols of success accepted by culture, society or even religious leaders.

Look at just part of the dreadful list he describes as "light afflictions:" labors; imprisonments; beaten times without number; in dangers; five times he received 39 lashes; thrice beaten with rods; once stoned; three times shipwrecked; hardships; sleepless nights; hunger and thirst; cold; homeless; wifeless; in weaknesses and difficulties.

Paul was betrayed, hated, rejected, insulted, persecuted and distressed. Like the other apostles and millions of Christians down through the ages, he eventually suffered martyrdom for his belief in Christ.

The Operation of Death

But in all his writings, Paul seems to accept this life of terrible suffering and sacrifice as normal and necessary. "Death works in us," he reasoned, that life might come to others.

I will never forget the day I learned the meaning of these words.

Every year we try to take small groups of American leaders to visit native missionary teams in India and other critical Asian nations. On one such trip, Brother Moses Paulose welcomed our group at the airport. One look convinced me that something was terribly wrong with him. He looked emaciated, weak and sick—especially next to the robust, overweight Americans.

"What's wrong, brother?" I asked.

He answered with just one sentence: "Death works in me, and life in them."

Tears came uncontrollably to my eyes as I recognized the allusion to Paul's rationale for suffering in 2 Corinthians 4:12. I discovered that Brother Paulose had been traveling to visit the missionaries without proper food and rest for nearly a month. He was just skin and bones!

He was making a conscious choice to deny the normal, minimum needs of his body for the sake of others' souls. For life to come to one, death must come to another. This is the biblical exchange from Genesis to Revelation. Somebody always pays the price, entering into the fellowship of Christ's sufferings. That's the way the Gospel is always pioneered into new areas, unreached villages and lost tribes. As valuable as broadcasting and literature are, they are only long-range artillery in this war. The foot soldier of the cross must always go in to establish the church by self-sacrifice and suffering. The exchange must take place.

Paul writes, "We are troubled on every side, yet not distressed; we are perplexed, but not in despair; persecuted, but not forsaken; cast down, but not destroyed; always bearing about in the body the dying of the Lord Jesus, that the life also of Jesus might be made manifest in our body ... So then death worketh in us, but life in you." (2 Corinthians 4:8-10,12)

Suffering at All Times

This concept of accepting suffering as a normal part of our everyday experience is resisted in the West. We're taught just the opposite. Everything in our culture, personal lives and churches is geared to avoid sacrifice and suffering. We believe that we must wait for a disaster or a time of tribulation to suffer, that sacrifice and self-denial are only reserved for special, temporary situations.

But that's not the way anything works in real life—not in the church or the world.

We celebrate the dedication of Olympic athletes who diet and train and exercise daily for years in order to prepare for the games. They give up not only physical comfort but any hope of a normal social and family life.

When police officers or fire fighters die, thousands often turn out for their funerals. We honor our children who die in military service in much the same way—often arranging public ceremonies and holidays. The Vietnam Memorial in Washington is considered one of the most popular tourist sites in the United States.

We expect TV celebrities such as actors, news correspondents and musicians to sacrifice any kind of normal life in order to entertain us around the clock—and they are paid millions of dollars to do so.

The names of astronauts become household words because they risk their lives in order to forward the conquest of space.

But the minute a Christian young person starts to fast and pray, consider the mission field, or give up career or romance for Christ—concerned counselors, family and friends will spend hours trying to keep him or her from "going off the deep end on this religious stuff." Even devout Christian parents will oppose Christian service when their own son or daughter is about to give up all for Christ.

Discipline, pain, sacrifice and suffering are rewarded with fame and fortune in the world. Why then do we refuse to accept it as a normal part of giving spiritual birth in the kingdom of our Lord?

The biblical requirement is that we should voluntarily go out of our way to accept assignments that involve suffering. But this teaching has been so long neglected that even the sound of it has become strange to our ears.

Living for Another Dimension

One of the secrets of accepting this life of voluntary suffering is a firm belief in the resurrection and eternity in the next world. Paul was willing to die because he lived unashamedly for another world. He writes, "We look not at the things which are seen, but at the things which are not seen: for the things which are seen are temporal; but the things which are not seen are eternal." (2 Corinthians 4:18)

How many of us need to confess our adulterous love affair with this present world? We cannot go on with God into the promised land because we're still looking back at the flesh-pots of Egypt.

Sometimes this sin is revealed in the big things, but much more often it is in the little things.

For example, I love a certain brand of perfumed soap. For years I always bought this brand. I considered it an innocent matter, until one day my wife pointed out that it was four times the price of generic soap. We could save $4 to $5 a month or $60 a year if I would switch brands. That money could be used to give the Gospel to thousands of people if we invested it wisely. I would be just as clean, but I would have to give up my special liking for that brand of soap. How could I reject such a justified rebuke?

If we can only start to make sacrifices in the small things like this, then it will be much easier to say no to the world and the flesh when we have to make big decisions.

Chapter 10

One-Way Ticket

Recently I counseled a couple planning to enter missionary service. They claimed they desperately wanted to serve the Lord. They were well-qualified, and it was obvious that the Holy Spirit was calling them into the privilege of His service.

But the world had a grip on them. They began to ask what I now recognize as the critical American questions about Christian service. If they went into missions, how would they live? Would they have a home? Would they have a retirement plan? What about the education of their children? What about insurance?

They were measuring the opportunity for service by the amount of inconvenience it would cause them. They didn't want to face the possibility of difficulties, sorrows, sacrifice and uncertainty in missionary service. The risks were too great, and so—like millions of other North Americans—they have not yet obeyed that call. They probably never will.

What a contrast with the routine sacrifices made by so many Christian workers in the Third World. I think of a team of five young pioneer missionaries whom the Lord had called to begin a mission in Rajasthan, a north Indian state. They had no money for train fare, let alone for food or rent. Everyone discouraged them and begged them to stay home. But this was their answer: "If we have no money to go by train, we will walk (1,500 miles). If one of us becomes sick and dies on the way, we will bury him on the roadside, and the rest of us will continue on. If only one of us survives the journey and reaches Rajasthan, and places only one Gospel tract on the hot desert sand of that state before he dies, we will have fulfilled our mission, and we will have obeyed our Lord."

One-Way Ticket to Kathmandu

Many others have left south India to go north on one of the famous one-way missionary tickets to Rajasthan or Nepal. These brothers and sisters leave all, knowing that they have no way to come home if God doesn't supply. They trust God to meet every need, conscious that the decision could mean starvation, sickness and death if He doesn't.

The Orient is filled with the graves of American and British missionaries from past generations who went out to the field, knowing full well that it was unlikely that they would ever return.

Some, like the Moravian brethren, sold themselves into slavery in order to enter closed lands. One couple voluntarily entered exile in a leper colony, knowing that it would cost them their freedom and eventually their lives.

As we read the stories of missionary heroes, there is a tendency to dismiss their sacrifices as something that can only happen in another place and time. But that just isn't true. If we permit the Lord to lead us, He will allow us to share in the fellowship of His sufferings wherever we are.

For example, all across the United States and Canada, there are quiet men and women working behind the scenes at secular jobs—but living to help support missions. They cannot go personally, but they are able to sponsor others. I think these are the real unsung heroes of missions today. Often they are known only to God. These are the people who willingly sacrifice to save a few dollars here and a few dollars there for the work of the Lord. They may get no glory in this world, but the Bible says they are serving Christ as effectively as any frontline warrior; and they are promised their reward.

There are many practical ways that we can enter into this fellowship of suffering without leaving the shores of North America. Wherever you are, there is a cross for you to bear. God has a path of sacrifice for each one of us if we will ask Him for the privilege of self-denial.

The Time and Money Test

Sacrifice and suffering for Christ all depend on how we choose to give our time and finances. Every one of us can at least find ways to give more time and more money to the kingdom of God if we will review our lifestyles.

The first step usually involves giving up the normal demands of our bodies for food and sleep in order to pray for others—situations, countries, peoples, tribes and the missionaries who are reaching out to them.

By fasting for a meal or giving up an evening of television, it is remarkable how much time you can make for the work of world-changing intercessory prayer. There are other strategic ways, of course, to volunteer time for missions, but none as important as the work of prayer.

When asked to give for missions, most of us feel that we're giving all we can. But by making a decision to look for ways to plan an act of sacrifice, there is almost always a way that we can give more.

Our home team in Carrollton, Texas, receives hundreds of letters from Christians who have found unique ways to help support native missionaries financially:

• A teenager in Milwaukee, Wisconsin, walks to school rather than purchase a bicycle. Instead of the new bike his parents had promised him for his birthday, he asked his mom and dad to send the money to the mission field. There it was used to purchase a bike for a native missionary.

• An executive in Dallas, Texas, "brown-bags" his lunch rather than go out to restaurants. The money he saves is more than enough to fully support a native missionary.

• A housewife in Arizona baby-sits for neighborhood

children and gives all the money to sponsor a Bible teacher.

• A retired missionary couple is able to sponsor several missionaries by selling vegetables from their garden to neighbors.

• A widow in Jamestown, New York, makes and sells quilts. The proceeds are used to sponsor her native missionaries.

• Another retired widow in Puerto Rico skips meals in order to send some of her tiny income for God's work.

There are probably thousands of other ways that can be found to create some extra dollars to help reach lost souls. I have long believed that almost every Christian in North America can find a way to help send out a native missionary by sacrificing somewhere in his or her personal lifestyle.

Become an Advocate for the Lost

Another method of sacrificial involvement is to become an advocate of world evangelization in your home, church and community. Sometimes this involves sacrificing some of your hopes and dreams for your children, church or civic organization. Often it means giving up prestige.

Spectator Christians and the people of this world have little time to encourage the volunteer for missions. Sometimes you will be misunderstood, deserted, hated or persecuted by others when you speak out for Christ.

In an age of plastic Christianity, when information is substituted for action, don't be surprised if your voluntary service for missions meets opposition. Respond as Christ did and thank God for the opportunity to be misunderstood.

Here are some of the practical ways you can become an advocate of missions in your locality:

• Become a distributor of publications from missionary organizations in your church and community.

• Arrange a weekly prayer meeting for missions in your home or support an existing prayer meeting with your attendance.

• Help arrange for your church, Sunday school class or club to sponsor a missionary as a group.

• Become active in increasing the percentage of your church

and denominational budget which is sent to frontline, native missions.

• Arrange for native missionary films, videos and speakers to come to your church and Christian organizations.

• Gently help your spouse and children to become more aware of native missions and find ways to join you in your ministry of sacrifice and suffering.

Smashing Your Vessel in His Service

When Gideon and his 300 mighty men attacked the Midianite hoards, they had to smash their earthen vessels in order to confuse the enemy with the sudden light.

I'm convinced that this is what Paul had in mind when he referred to the treasure we hold in our earthen vessels, in 2 Corinthians 4:7,8.

We must be willing to let our lives be broken and smashed in order for this light to break out. And we don't naturally want that, of course. We want to admire our vessels and show off how clever and talented and valuable we are.

But Jesus insisted that there is no life unless first the seed is planted in the ground and dies. There is no experience of the Christ-life without the cross, no power released unless we risk suffering and sacrifice.

If Jesus Christ Himself learned obedience through suffering, how dare we try squirm out of accepting this as a normal part of our Christian lives? Excuses won't do. None of us is too old or too young to learn the power of voluntary self-denial. We can never say we've suffered enough already or that we're not called to sacrifice. The Bible does not leave us this option. We must come to that place in which suffering is normal.

When we learn to run to it and embrace it, when we can plan habitually to go without things for Christ's sake, then we've begun to live the life of reasonable service: "I beseech you therefore, brethren, by the mercies of God, that ye present your bodies a living sacrifice, holy, acceptable unto God, which is your reasonable service." (Romans 12:1)

Chapter 11

Be Holy As I Am Holy

As the night fell, I sat with a frustrated pastor and his wife, sensing the agony and heart cry of his soul. In their dining room that Sunday evening, we stirred our coffee and stared out the window in strained silence. All I could see was the pitch black night. And as it turned out, that night was symbolic of so many of the lives of people in his church.

Like many other pastors who have shared their private pains with me over the years, this brother had just unburdened his heart about the tragic situation in his congregation. Although outwardly his people seemed like a vibrant and growing church, beneath the surface they were full of confusion—blinded by sin, having no understanding of what it means to follow the Holy One of Israel.

The pastor himself was confused and concerned, and explained that he felt like a hypocrite. He claimed he was tempted to pack up and walk away from it all. But where would he go and was that the Lord's solution? He had many questions, and I had few answers.

It was a fairly large church of a major denomination, and nobody would have guessed that there was anything wrong. I had preached in the church that morning, and I was impressed. The hymns were meaningfully and vibrantly sung. Everything appeared normal. But in reality, he insisted, it was all a sham.

"Brother K.P.," said the pastor, "I am tired and desperate—I stand before these people and preach Sunday after Sunday. Yet there is no real difference between them and the people of the world. Right now, we have every sin you can imagine going on openly among the believers in our congregation—divorce, adultery, gossip, lust-filled lives, unforgiveness, pride, boasting, jealousy, lack of self-control, rebellious youth.

"I don't know if I can go on preaching the Word to such hardened hearts."

He continued, not waiting for a reply. "Brother, is this really the church of Christ, or are we just calling it the church because of our traditions and history?"

Plainly, he seemed a hungry soul, not satisfied with living a lie. He said he was fed up with putting on a front, tired of just fulfilling the expectations of his denominational traditions, pleasing men and church boards without seeing reality in the lives of the people.

I'm sorry to say that today this dear pastor is no longer there; he has walked away from a successful pulpit and career in his denomination. He is willing to be unknown, choosing instead to spend time waiting upon the living God—walking before Him with a blameless heart.

How many pastors, I wonder, would do the same thing if they were honest about the true spiritual condition of the people in their congregations?

A Masterful Deception

As we look at so many of our churches today, we are not seeing the real body of Christ at all, but a masterful deception. Often, the doctrine seems proper—solidly evangelical and correct.

Some of the largest church buildings and biggest congregations in history are springing up. Big names, huge choirs, flashy advertising and the power of television cause us to believe that we are seeing something really great. But we must challenge these notions. All is not what it appears to be.

Just the opposite may be true. Tell me why churches have sought after entertainment, recreation and social activities to keep people in their congregations? One pastor recently boasted in a national news-weekly that his church had a better recreation facility than any commercial health club in town. It cost them millions of dollars, and the pastor claimed they had the best equipment available. It's difficult to believe he was serious. Since when did matching the devil in facilities become part of the Great Commission?

Meanwhile, counseling ministries are proliferating like wildfire because the lives of so many Christians are empty and confused. They cannot find answers in their church. So now, they are going outside the local church. Radio and TV ministries are bombarded with letters and calls from families and individuals who don't have solutions to their spiritual needs and problems.

Our churches often are bursting at the seams; we have programs every night of the week, but we lack the power and authority of a life in tune with the will of God.

Our lives are so contrary to the holiness and purity that God seeks from His people that we have become easy marks for the attacks of Satan and demons. While worshipping God with our lips, our lives are growing further and further away from His Word.

False Gospels; False Christs

The New Testament warns us that in the end times, there will be those who will come teaching a gospel that is not the Gospel at all; presenting a "christ" that is not Christ (2 Corinthians 11:4).

And I believe that what we see already happening today—and much more that will soon come upon us—is a direct result of the past decades of false teaching. We have been brainwashed with what Dietrich Bonhoeffer originally called the "cheap grace" gospel. As a result we are in ruin in our individual lives and families, as well as in our churches.

I fear for the nation and people whose Christian churches have forsaken holiness and separation from sin and the world.

This is a new gospel which is really half of the Gospel. It correctly portrays the wonderful love and forgiveness of God, but it downplays the need for confession, repentance and changed living. Most of all, it virtually ignores the ongoing work of the cross in our everyday lives.

Because of it, we are now blinded to hundreds of scriptures that teach practical holiness in everyday living. This false gospel ignores the very teachings of our Lord and Savior! Jesus said, "Blessed are the pure in heart: for they shall see God." (Matthew 5:8)

This means you may go forward in every meeting, read all the Bible you want, and study all the theology you can and be in church every time the door opens—but you still won't be able to stand before God on judgment day. The Bible says that the only way to see the face of the living God is to be pure and to be purged from sin in your heart.

This is the fact that is lost in the "cheap grace" gospel that has flooded our churches. And today, we are seeing the terrible fruit of this watered-down perversion of the truth—*the world has swallowed up the church*. Most Christians are living carnal lives of defeat and failure.

God's Unchanging Desire for the Church

The Bible says the Lord Jesus Christ is coming for a bride that is holy and pure and spotless. He is not coming for a harlot church. He is coming for a holy people who are walking the narrow road as He walked.

I believe Revelation 18:4 is a very relevant verse to our churches today. Listen to it, "Come out of her, my people, that ye be not partakers of her sins, and that ye receive not of her plagues."

God is calling for total separation and holy living from His people—just as He always has throughout every generation and dispensation. God does not change. The commandment the Lord gives to His people is always to be "holy because I am holy."

From the beginning of creation, God's desire has been to have a holy people. We are impressed with size and quantity, but God is immensely more concerned about the quality. We are living in such a statistics-conscious society that will do almost anything for bigger numbers, larger organizations and mega-churches. But all the while God is looking for a few who will walk in purity and holiness.

He simply is not impressed with the length of our lists and the size of our directories. Oh, that God would help us to see that we're less than the size of germs in His vast universe. Yet we go on measuring the effectiveness of our businesses, careers and ministries in terms of bigger and bigger budgets, more influential friends and larger buildings.

Even our Christian magazines are full of photographs and numbers designed to show how great we think we are. If we could only see what a tragic joke all this is to God. We've become just like the secular culture around us, blinded by the god of this world—Satan himself. We are seeking to gratify the lusts of our flesh and of the mind as lost sinners do, comparing ourselves with ourselves.

In the Old Testament we read God's criticism against Israel was not that they were not offering large enough offerings in terms of size or number, but that their offerings were impure. (Malachi 1:6-11) What God is looking for is true holiness and purity, separation from the world and sin.

God had sent prophet after prophet to Israel—for 1,450 years—calling them to turn from sin to purity, but they had not listened. Israel's lack of reverence was manifested in their bringing to the Lord offerings of animals that were sick, lame and blind. They offered Him less than their best. Much of what believers offer Him today falls into the same category. There is often little self-denial or sacrifice involved in what we are bringing before Him. Our lives are mixed up with the ways of this world, crippled by our disobedience and deceit—unworthy of His call on us.

In Romans 12:1,2, we read of the pure offering God seeks today. He wants our very lives—set apart from the world, self and sin.

In Isaiah 1:11-17, God asks His people, "To what purpose is the multitude of your sacrifices unto me? saith the Lord: I am full of the burnt offerings of rams, and the fat of fed beasts; and I delight not in the blood of bullocks, or of lambs, or of he goats. When ye come to appear before me, who hath required this at your hand, to tread my courts? Bring no more vain oblations; incense is an abomination unto me; the new moons and sabbaths, the calling of assemblies, I cannot away with; it is iniquity, even the solemn meeting. Your new moons and your appointed feasts my soul hateth: they are a trouble unto me; I am weary to bear them. And when ye spread forth your hands, I will hide mine eyes from you: yea, when ye make many prayers, I will not hear: your hands are full of blood. Wash you, make you clean; put away the evil of your doings from before mine eyes; cease to do evil; Learn to do well; seek judgment, relieve the oppressed, judge the fatherless, plead for the widow."

From the book of Genesis to the book of Revelation, we see this one message God continues to impress upon us. He is looking for a holy people with a pure heart. Righteousness is critically important to Him because He is righteous—and He is never satisfied with less than a righteous people.

Chapter 12

Battle Lines Must Be Drawn

I will never forget staying with a family as I was traveling to preach in conferences here in the United States. As I went to bed that night in the room that was given to me by this family, I discovered for some reason I could not sleep. I felt as though I were in a haunted house. I began to have nightmares, and soon a terrible and unreasonable fear gripped me. In a short time, I woke up and realized I was under attack by what the New Testament calls the fiery darts of the wicked one.

I was not alone in my room, but demon spirits were attacking me. Recognizing Satan as my enemy, I rebuked him in the name of Jesus and eventually went back to sleep.

The next morning I got up, and I heard a demonic rock and roll beat coming out of the room next to me. The door was open, and I looked in as I walked by.

I was shocked to see, plastered all over the walls in that room, many lewd posters of rock stars. Some were half naked, and others were dressed in leather and chains. From the very expressions of arrogance and sinful pride on their faces, I could see that the pictures resembled idols of the demon gods worshipped in the darkest temples of Asia!

The room belonged to the teenager of the family. All of a sudden it dawned on me why I had to face such a spiritual battle in order to sleep the night before.

Here was a Christian teenager, unknowingly adoring and worshipping demon gods. Yet this was the same family that I went to church with during their missions conference. They sat in the pews and were partaking in the whole service. It looked all so good, as if they were really committed Christians; and I'm sure that they considered themselves in harmony with the true God. Yet their home was under demonic power!

How many millions of our Christian homes are similarly enslaved? How many call themselves Christians, yet their homes are trampled over by the powers of darkness? The lives of so many youth are being destroyed and derailed before they even know what has happened. Suddenly, they find themselves enslaved to alcohol, drugs, immorality and all kinds of lusts for material things—for fame—and for power.

Millions of beautiful, bright Christian teenagers are being destroyed today—just at the moment in life when they should be launching out into lifetimes of productive Christian service.

In Christian homes untold hours are being spent worshipping before the TV idol. Through the advertising and programming, every kind of wickedness and vice is coming into our minds and lifestyles. The media is developing appetites in the hearts of Christians which give footholds for demons to control and ruin precious lives. Christian mothers and fathers should have discernment to see what Satan is doing to their children. But the god of this world has blinded their eyes. Indeed most Christians are so far away from God that they no longer seem to be able to see the devil in the art, music, fashion and pop culture of our day.

Through the medium of television, many Christians are letting down the barriers of separation and holiness which should be protecting their lives and families from the attacks of the evil one. Their homes have become dens of Satan, and their minds and morals are the next things that go. This is the story of all sin and spiritual defeat. The Bible faithfully records it from the garden of Eden until the end of time.

The Urgent Need for Restoration

Where are the fathers who will stand against this flood of uncleanness and say, "As for me and my house, we will serve the Lord?" (Joshua 24:15) Where are the mothers of Titus 2:3-5, women that "be in behaviour as becometh holiness," who "teach the young women" to live godly lives as well? Where are children who remember to honor and obey their parents?

We must choose to restore holiness to our families as well as our personal lives and churches.

Holiness is not a gift of the Spirit. It is not a feeling that comes mysteriously over us. It is not something that God does to us. It begins with a deliberate choice—an act of the will. The seed we sow will come up and produce the fruit of holiness as the end result.

Battle lines must be drawn in our lives and in the lives of those we are commanded to protect. It is vitally important for every reader of this book to embrace this responsibility as his or her own.

And I am especially concerned that those of us in positions of leadership take the responsibility to purify our own individual lives and homes. If we don't, how can we minister holiness to others whom we counsel?

In Ezekiel 34:2,3, God speaks clearly, "Son of man, prophesy against the shepherds of Israel, prophesy, and say unto them, Thus saith the Lord God unto the shepherds; Woe be to the shepherds of Israel that do feed themselves! should not the shepherds feed the flocks? Ye eat the fat, and ye clothe you with the wool, ye kill them that are fed: but ye feed not the flock."

Like never before, we need godly shepherds who will cry out against sin and call God's people to repentance, to live holy, separate lives.

As we read through the Old Testament, how often do we find God pronouncing judgment against the false shepherds who are scattering the flock and destroying their lives? In Matthew 7:15, Jesus warned of false teachers who come in sheep's clothing, but actually they are wolves. The greatest tragedy in this land today, I believe, is that pulpits are filled with men who are speaking their own words and do not have a word from the Lord. They flatter their congregations with words in order to fulfill their selfish ambitions in the flesh.

When our motives are mixed and our personal lives are filled with hidden sins, the powers of darkness have a direct inroad into our ministries. They can thus control our thoughts and words, bringing death to individual lives, congregations and ministries.

Such a minister is defenseless in spiritual warfare. He will welcome the thoughts and suggestions of the enemy and do everything to build his own reputation. At the same time, he will water down God's Word and will back off from anything that is of serious consequence, such as preaching against sin, or confronting a brother or sister who has fallen into error, or calling his people to a life of separation and holiness. He can easily be deceived into misunderstanding God's blessings, even taking pride in the size of buildings, the number of people in his congregation or the size of his church budget. The approval of men, big titles and popularity can simply take over his whole heart and mind.

Paul, speaking to the Thessalonians, tells them: "We were bold in our God to speak unto you the gospel of God with much contention. For our exhortation was not of deceit, nor of uncleanness, nor in guile: But as we were allowed of God to be put in trust with the gospel, even so we speak; not as pleasing men, but God, which trieth our hearts. For neither at any time used we flattering words, as ye know, nor a cloak of covetousness; God is witness: Nor of men sought we glory." (1 Thessalonians 2:2-6)

In Jeremiah 10:21, we read, "For the pastors are become brutish, and have not sought the Lord: therefore they shall not prosper, and all their flocks shall be scattered." In Jeremiah

12:10, the prophet continues, "Many pastors have destroyed my vineyard, they have trodden my portion under foot, they have made my pleasant portion a desolate wilderness."

This, I believe, is the sad picture of what we all too often are seeing in our churches today.

As never before, we need God's servants who are willing to risk their lives to preach the uncompromising Word of God, calling people once again to total separation and purity in their lives.

As lay Christians, we need to seek out courageous shepherds like this and put ourselves under their ministries. We need to encourage them, pray for them and submit to them as Paul urged in Hebrews 13:17, "For they watch for your souls."

Chapter 13

At the Crossroads

Today we all stand at the crossroads on the question of personal holiness. Each of us must make the choice about which way we are going to go. This isn't a choice only preachers or Christian leaders must make, although I pray that it will start there. No, every believing man, woman, boy and girl must decide personally.

"Will I surrender to the spirit of our age, or resist and join the company of overcomers?" is the question to ask.

Do we want to continue to live in defeat, failure and un-righteousness? Or will we decide to follow the path of excellence that leads to quality of life, inward purity and separation unto God?

Of course, we also can continue in a life of hypocrisy and legalism and be content to put on an external show of right-eousness.

Even if we are able to fool others for a time with religious sham, we cannot lie to God for even an instant. If, after seeing clearly God's desire for us to live a life of purity and holiness, we still do not obey and commit our lives, the Bible tells us in Revelation 22:11,12 that God will not always strive with us but come with judgment. "He that is unjust, let him be unjust still: and he which is filthy, let him be filthy still: and he that is righteous, let him be righteous still: and he that is holy, let him be holy still. And, behold, I come quickly; and my reward is with me, to give every man according as his work shall be."

The Bible tells us in 1 Corinthians 3:13 and 4:5 that "every man's work shall be made manifest: for the day shall declare it, because it shall be revealed by fire; and the fire shall try every man's work of what sort it is .... Therefore judge nothing before the time, until the Lord come, who both will bring to light the hidden things of darkness, and will make manifest the counsels of the hearts: and then shall every man have praise of God."

We must realize that while God really wants us to be shining lights in this world, winning the lost and making an impact upon our generation or religious activism can never substitute for a separated life.

But let us remember that it is equally important that we are not offering service to God in the power of the flesh, with an impure heart. All the work and sacrifice we accomplish—even in the cause of world evangelism—can never be pleasing to the Lord unless it is done from a pure and holy heart.

No wonder the writer of Hebrews warns us to "serve God acceptably with reverence and godly fear: For our God is a consuming fire." (Hebrews 12:28,29)

The Dangers of Legalism

You now may be saying, "That sounds like legalism to me." I assure you it is not. We must stop confusing obedience to God with legalism. We must stop confusing holiness with legalism.

There is a very real danger of legalism—but that's not what the Bible is talking about here. Jesus hated legalism and rebuked legalists in some of the strongest language He ever used. But He also taught obedience, holiness, purity and separation.

Let's define legalism in biblical terms. Legalism is obeying the teachings of men as the Pharisees did, adding human rules and standards of behavior onto what God has given. Obedience to the Word of God is different altogether. It comes out of a true commitment and genuine love for the Lord. It is not based on external things and following the interpretations of men.

This is the reason why the Lord Jesus Christ frequently told His audience that to follow Him meant they would have to walk with Him as He walked. He said, "No man can serve two masters." (Matthew 6:24) To live for Jesus and follow Him, you must give up your own desires and wishes for your life. That's what we need today so desperately.

There are two sure ways to avoid legalism.

First, we must stop comparing our lives with others. This can happen anywhere, even in the best churches and organizations, and it is a terrible sin. Instead, we must bring our lives before the light of His Word. We must yearn to become like Jesus. We must take our eyes off ourselves—and others—and gaze at Him. He alone becomes our standard.

Second, I urge you not to be satisfied with fulfilling externals that may be prescribed by your denomination, fellowship, organization or any other traditions of men. Again, you must pursue knowing the Lord Jesus Christ. Learning all about Jesus and His teachings and theology is not what I am talking about. You must spend time with the Lord Himself and learn to know Him personally in your spirit. Fall in love with Him, and get to know Him intimately. You'll find as you do this that you can obey all that He commands without any danger of falling into legalism.

Steps to Holiness

For many, entering into a life of holiness and separation unto the Lord may appear to be a mystery. But this need not be so. Like all the other blessings and requirements in the Christian's life, all it requires is a simple act of faith.

The first step of entering into holy living is to rediscover the full work of the cross. God has provided not only for us to be saved from the penalty of sin on Calvary, but He also provided for us to have victory over sin on a day-to-day basis. Every Christian needs to study this great truth in Romans 6 through 8 until it becomes reality in his or her daily life. The normal Christian life God has ordained for each of us is one of triumph over the world, the flesh and the devil.

To begin living this pure, separated lifestyle, we must recognize we are not our own, that we are bought with a price; and blood was the price the Lord paid for us. He has purchased us and has a right to control us in the same sense a slave has no right to his own life. A believer must come to the place of reckoning he is totally dead with Christ—crucified with Him and living no more for self. Now we live every minute and second to please our Master. We are His; we belong to Him, body and soul and spirit.

Second, holiness requires waiting on God. Without spending time in the presence of the Holy One, no one can become holy—for God alone is the source of all holiness. We need to control our TV sets and the other idols that are binding us and keeping us away from the presence of the Lord and His written Word. Give up the secret sins that are enslaving you, and reclaim the areas in your life that have been given over to the enemy.

Put Satan on notice that all the claims he has on your life have been settled by Christ's blood on the cross and that you have recognized you are free from sin. Tell him you have turned yourself completely over to the Lord.

Third, confess and repent from all known sin. Be sure you have purged yourself from any claims the enemy still might have on you through habits in your life. Make a list of everything the Holy Spirit brings to your mind, small or big, that you need to turn away from. These could be people or habits or even your thought life and that which feeds it such as books, catalogs and videos. Anything the Holy Spirit brings to your mind must go. Give the Lord time to turn His spotlight on those areas that are keeping you from growing closer to Him.

A year ago, I did a series of broadcasts aired from Sri Lanka called "The Changes That Take Place When Jesus Comes to Our Home." Day after day, for 50 days, I asked my audience to think in terms of living their lives as though Christ Himself had actually come to live with them. How differently we would live if Jesus in human form were sitting and walking with us every moment of the day!

Tens of thousands of people wrote in and told of the radical changes that took place in their lives as they began to live consciously, imagining in their mind's eye that Jesus Christ was actually living with them.

The truth is, of course, the Lord Jesus is living in us by His Holy Spirit. He is with us always. We have no plans which are secret to Him. He sees us when we turn from Him and choose sin.

Yet how tragic it is when God's people indulge themselves in sins of any kind, grieving the very heart of the Lord Jesus Christ. The Bible clearly says in 1 John 2:6, "He that saith he abideth in him ought himself also so to walk, even as he walked." Again, 1 John 3:5,6 states, "... in him is no sin. Whosoever abideth in him sinneth not."

For most modern Christians, living as if verses like these are not even in the Bible, the concept of holiness seems strange and alien—something archaic or left over from another era. But for those who seek spiritual reality, it is past time to recover this doctrine.

Chapter 14

Spiritual Intimacy

I'll never forget one of my first prayer meetings in America. I had been in the United States for only a few weeks, and I was eager to meet the spiritual giants and leaders. Even before leaving India, I had heard of one man in particular. He was famous for his uncompromising defense of the Scriptures and sound doctrine.

So on that first Sunday, I hurried to visit his church—one of the most famous in the city. More than 3,000 attended the morning services to hear the talented choirs and outstanding preaching of the Word.

My ears perked right up when the pastor of the church announced a special emphasis at the upcoming mid-week prayer meeting. There were some things "heavy on his heart," he said. He announced the name of a certain chapel, and I determined to attend.

In other parts of the world, where Christians are often persecuted and attacked for their faith, prayer meetings are the very centerpiece of the church calendar. Everyone attends. Prayer and worship often last long into the night. Prayer is the powerhouse of their faith, and many believers rise before dawn for daily prayer meetings.

Prayer is probably the best thermometer you will ever have to measure your growth in Christ. It drives all that is truly spiritual, both in our church and personal lives.

On the appointed night I arrived early, fearful that I would not get a good seat—or even a seat at all! Right away I noticed that there was room for about 500 worshippers, but there was no singing or clapping. The hall was completely empty. I walked all the way to the front and took a seat to wait.

By 7:15 I was getting really worried. "I must have gotten the wrong hall," I reasoned. I went outside to check the name above the door, but it was the chapel where I had been waiting.

Finally, at 7:30 several others came into the huge hall. There were no leader, songs or worship. People sat and talked about sports and the weather.

After about 45 minutes an elderly man came in to lead the prayer meeting. The pastor was not even there. I counted seven people. The elderly man read a scripture, made some devotional observations and led a brief prayer.

As the others got up to leave, I sat stunned. Was this it? Weren't they going to stay and wait upon God? Where was the worship? The tears? The cries for guidance and direction? Where was the list of the sick, and the poor, and those in need? What about that burden that pastor said was heavy on his heart? Weren't we going to intercede for a miracle?

And what about the missions? I asked myself silently. This church supported missions on every continent. Weren't they going to pass around the missionary prayer letters and pray together for those facing attacks from Satan on the front lines?

Many set up their churches and lives very much like their secular businesses and careers. With or without the blessing and presence of God, religion goes on like a well-oiled machine.

These churches, by the tens of thousands, have what are called "mid-week prayer meetings." But it's a shame to even call them prayer meetings. What really happens seldom has anything to do with prayer at all! The people gather. Someone stands to lead some singing. Then *one* person prays—briefly.

Another person reads a list of announcements. Of course, the preacher usually delivers a short homily. In some cases, there may then be a few prayers, but most close having had no real time of prayer at all. How can we call that a prayer meeting?

Nothing reveals the bankruptcy of modern Christianity more clearly and quickly than the current crisis in prayer. It has reached emergency proportions and demands our attention.

I Can Handle It Myself, Thank You!

Many times, I have asked, "Why is it that we as believers in the West do not pray more?" and "Why is it churches do not give more attention to prayer?"

After all, since prayer is the ultimate act of spiritual intimacy with God, shouldn't it be the central activity of our whole lives? It cannot be that we lack teaching on prayer. Few Christians have more books and seminars on prayer than do the believers of North America.

The awful truth, whether we admit it or not, is that we don't pray because in our hearts we don't think we really need God. We don't know how to pray because true prayer can only originate from a life emptied of self-sufficiency.

The church we see today is truly the church of Laodicea described in Revelation 3:14-22. There is no more accurate description of our spiritual condition anywhere in the Bible. Jesus said of this church, "I know thy works, that thou art neither cold nor hot: I would thou wert cold or hot. So then because thou art lukewarm, and neither cold nor hot, I will spue thee out of my mouth. Because thou sayest, I am rich, and increased with goods, and have need of nothing; and knowest not that thou art wretched, and miserable, and poor, and blind, and naked ..." (Revelation 15-17)

Our prayerlessness highlights our self-sufficiency. This I-can-handle-it-myself mindset is the spiritual cancer of our times. It is the root cause of the present powerlessness both in our personal lives and our churches. Because we have not yet comprehended the essence of prayer, we fail to see the arrogance and terrible rebellion of our present state.

We have so much else to depend on today—buildings, machines, money, programs and technology. We spend thousands of hours with consultants in study and planning. Yet there seems to be no time to pray.

Clearly, we have lost touch with the eternal, living God. Instead, we are serving the machines, programs and systems that we have established. But they are idols, gods that we have created and now control with our own ingenuity. And the message of the Bible on idolatry is clear. Either we will turn from these idols and trust in God, or the Lord Himself will intervene to destroy the works of our flesh. It is dangerous to travel on in this pathway of pride—in our personal lives as well as our church lives.

Waiting for Power From Above

How different our current lifestyle is from the instructions of Christ to the first disciples.

After three and a half years of constant example and teaching, what was the only lesson He wanted them to remember? "Without Me you can do nothing!" No wonder He told them to tarry in Jerusalem and wait until they were endowed with power from above, before they went out to fulfill the Great Commission. He wanted them to realize that, in and of themselves, they were headed for disaster.

Unless we come to this place of total helplessness, we can never understand prayer. This is why Paul says "When I am weak, then I am strong." Prayer is nothing more than voicing our dependence upon God. And the answer to every prayer is nothing more than this: God is with us, in all His power and authority, to make up for our human limitations.

Each of us, in our own personal daily walk and work, is led through trials and tribulations. These test our faith and should spur us on to a life of more prayer and deeper dependence upon God.

We have countless opportunities to trust God in the world of missions work. However, even in this realm, where it would seem we would want to depend on God the most, it is rare to find leaders moving out in reliance upon the Lord.

I am amazed at the dozens of small and major missions conferences and consultations that go on annually in the United States and Canada. I have attended a few of them. Seldom have the leaders called for a non-stop, all-day prayer meeting for the needs of the lost world.

I have also talked to dozens of mission leaders and asked them how much time they spend in prayer with their staffs. With few exceptions, most do not even have a two-hour weekly prayer meeting. Yet these same leaders are crisscrossing the country to meet with consultants on fund raising and development.

We have time to study anthropology, sociology, theology, marketing and media, but we have no time to pray. It is nothing for our leaders to spend two or three days in continual planning and scheming. Yet you will seldom find these same men and women on their knees for one night of prayer. Why aren't we waiting for a revelation of His plan? Crying out for the invisible God to go before us into battle?

Is this not a clear indication these leaders and organizations are trying to reach the lost world without coming to grips with spiritual reality? How can we overcome unseen spiritual forces, cast down evil strongholds and open closed doors unless we are a people of prayer? God's army always moves forward on its knees.

Thousands of hidden people groups are still without the Gospel in Asia. Yet we go on blindly—holding planning conference after planning conference on how to reach them without at least giving equal time to prayer.

If our own careers, churches, families and ministries are not built on prayer, we are in danger of fathering an Ishmael.

Chapter 15

More Attitude
Than Action

In Genesis 17, God fulfills the promise He had given to Abraham in prayer. This is a powerful lesson revealing the absolute necessity of waiting for the Lord to act rather than relying on our own ingenuity.

God had promised Abraham and Sarah a child. But as the years went by, nothing happened. As the years of childbearing passed, they began to wonder how God could ever fulfill His promise. They reasoned and agonized for months, I'm sure, and finally decided that they had to give God a helping hand.

As a result of their own carnal reasonings, they did what a lot of us do today when we have a faith crisis—they came up with their own plan. It was to employ Sarah's servant girl Hagar as a surrogate mother. The child Abraham fathered by her was named Ishmael.

We don't like to admit it, but today this same kind of thing still happens—even in our church business meetings and missions work. In our fund-raising appeals, from the pulpit and in our communications, we are constantly being brainwashed that

God is depending on our efforts. If we let Him down, goes this kind of reasoning, His purpose will not be fulfilled.

We can't wait for God, so we do things our way. And then like Abraham, we seek God's blessings on our efforts.

After Ishmael was born, Abraham knew something was wrong so he sought God's approval and blessing. The God of mercy did answer Abraham's pleadings and blessed Ishmael in some ways—but He would not give Ishmael the promise. What's more, to this day, there is war between the children of Ishmael and the children of Isaac. So it is with all the problems of our flesh; how often they create more problems than the one we intended them to cure.

You see, God has never changed His plan. His work will always be carried out in the Spirit or it is not His work at all. "Not by might, nor by power, but by my spirit, saith the Lord of hosts." (Zechariah 4:6)

Ishmael had been born to Abraham when he was 86 years old. In Genesis 17:1 we find that Abraham is now 99 years old and obviously impotent. Now the chosen time has come for God to act. There was nothing left in Abraham—absolutely nothing—that could help him or Sarah to have a son. The Bible says she was 90, well past her childbearing years as well.

Isaac was to be born miraculously so all could see that this new race was a people of grace, created by the grace and mercy of God.

Then, in Genesis 17:11, God introduces a powerful symbol of Abraham's vulnerability. He instructs him to be circumcised. Later, Paul explains in Philippians 3:3 that we are the true circumcision because we have no confidence in the flesh.

The cutting off of the flesh was a dramatic demonstration to Abraham and his descendants that the people of God were to have no confidence in their own ability.

As God's people for this present age, we must also forsake our Ishmaels and be circumcised in our hearts. Only as we learn to depend on God will we father no more Ishmaels of our own. How dare we run to the world for their expertise as if

God is helpless to do His work? I am convinced that we have been deceived by the powers of darkness. For too many years, we've been transferring our faith from God to the methods of modern business, management, marketing and science.

No wonder we're not praying today. No wonder we're not spending nights in prayer waiting for God to show us His plan. No wonder the authority, power and glory of God are gone from our assemblies and missions. No wonder we're victims of every new fad, philosophy and pseudo-theology that comes along. Our dependency on self is producing a 20th century baby boom of Ishmaels.

Old Testament Saints Prayed Their Way to Victory

Throughout Scripture, we see that God used men and women who depended on Him. These humble people often changed the course of history, turned a generation to God and impacted their total environment. They illustrate vividly the power of a life connected to the Lord in prayer.

Moses led a people from slavery to nationhood. A renegade murderer, Moses learned the hard way to listen for the voice of God.

When he was first called, he mistakenly thought he was strong, educated and smart enough to free the Jews from slavery. But it took 40 years of waiting on God to bring him to the place where he would acknowledge there was nothing in him and his Egyptian education. He was so humbled by this point he was actually speechless.

But that is when the amazing prayer dialogue between God and Moses was able to begin. How many times in the life of Moses do we see him running to God for counsel and advice? How many times did he wait days and weeks before the Lord in prayer and fasting?

Moses was a man of intercession. He was always bringing his burden for the people of Israel before the Lord. The tragedy of our day is that so few have the burden to take on this priestly role.

God's answers to the prayers of Moses fill five books of the Bible. The Lord showed him that He was interested in every detail in the lives of His people. In these times of prayer, he was taught how to lead, organize and govern a people-— receiving minute instructions from God on hundreds of different subjects. And God revealed His glory and power through Moses. His God-given authority was backed with remarkable miracles.

Gideon learned to recognize the voice of God and received commands from God as he sought the Lord. Through fleeces, signs and messages from the Lord, Gideon whittled down an army of 32,000 to just 300 soldiers chosen of God. Again and again, the Lord made clear to him the reason for this strange tactic: "This I do so that they will not boast that they have done it."

Empowered by God, this tiny force miraculously defeated an army of 135,000! God was trying to show to Gideon and the Israeli forces His power. He knew his helplessness before the Lord and came again and again in prayer for guidance. In answer to those prayers, God Himself showed Gideon strategies, tactics and maneuvers that defeated a vastly superior force.

Elijah received supernatural strength and power. The Bible tells us that Elijah was very human, with the same passions and ego problems we have. Materially, he had nothing of this world: no home, no buildings, no publicity, no congregation, no food, no friends. So he had to depend completely and totally on God. Yet he was able to control the elements, raise the dead, call down fire from heaven and achieve great physical feats. There is power in prayer because it connects us to the source of all power.

Prophets like Isaiah and Jeremiah felt the passion of God's heart for His wayward people. Through prayerful dependence and waiting on the Lord, Isaiah and Jeremiah actually began to feel the pain of God's broken heart over His sinful and rebellious people. Jeremiah so entered into the heart of God that he could not re-strain the sobs and tears of grief. Prayer thus can become a very subjective thing as we emotionally enter into the heart and mind of Jesus. Their powerful prophecies revealed the love of God and His plan to punish and restore His fallen people. They cleansed, comforted and helped to restore a people who might otherwise have given up in despair.

Nehemiah is another example. As he heard stories of the grim ruins of Jerusalem, he did not run to fund-raising consultants for advice. He did not scheme and call for a conference of engineers and politicians. Instead, we read in the first chapter of his book that he wept and prayed months before the living God.

And God answered those prayers with a vision for a major public works project. A humble civil servant, Nehemiah waited on God for timing and favor to present the concept to a king who might otherwise have been hostile to the plan. In Jerusalem, he continued to commune with God through each step of the project. Through prayer, he received wisdom from above to mount a major political campaign, organize the reconstruction and deal with the enemies of God's people.

Prayer Power in the New Testament

The New Testament church was born in a prayer meeting at Pentecost. Jesus promised power to His church if they would but wait on Him. Paul's writings are filled with so many references to prayer it almost seems as if he spent his entire ministry simply praying from one city to the next!

But the awesome prayer life of the apostles and the early church was only a pale reflection of our Lord's devotion to prayer.

When we look at the life of our Lord Jesus, we are amazed at how important He considered prayer. He began His ministry with 40 days of fasting and prayer. At critical junctures, such as choosing the 12 disciples and before going to the cross—He spent whole nights in prayer. Jesus was forever withdrawing from the crowds to spend extended times alone with God the Father.

Yet, for Jesus, it was more than just spending time. Jesus not only made prayer a priority, but He modeled a life of constant prayer. Jesus demonstrated an attitude of prayer in His every action.

Jesus showed us true prayer is not found in any of the formulas to which we cling. In fact it is not necessarily even words or thoughts. Instead, prayer starts with what you are in your heart! It is more an attitude than action.

Effective, genuine prayer is a dialogue with God. It rolls together dependence, humility, obedience, submission and worship. Finally, it waits on God to display His grace and mercy.

Such prayers as these may burst forth with a single phrase or sentence. This is why the Lord Jesus would frequently lift His eyes to the Father and utter one-sentence prayers which brought instant answers—healed bodies and stilled storms.

More than by giving us a set of phrases and words, Jesus exemplified a moment-by-moment dependence on God in His prayer life. We have not learned to pray as Jesus taught us to until we have learned to *live prayerfully* as He did. His prayers sprung naturally and spontaneously out of a constant aware-ness of the Father's will. He enjoyed a well-practiced intimacy with the Father. He did not pray *to* God, but *with* God. Until we learn to pray with the Son in the same way He did with the Father, we have not learned the basic posture of prayer.

What Prayer Is Not

How different this kind of prayer is from the empty words, motions and fads that pass themselves off as prayer in so many of our lives today! Since the meaning of true prayer has become so distorted, it would be good for us to look here and in the next chapter at three things prayer is not:

True prayer is not magic. The sad reality is that many of our modern prayers are frequently little different from Hindu *mantras*.

Throughout the pagan world, some form of a *shaman*, or witch doctor, is always called in times of trouble. Perhaps it is for sickness, drought or famine. Or it might be a business or family problem. A fee is paid, and the priest will then utter *mantras* in hopes that the victim's "luck" will change. These can go on for hours as the medium seeks to contact various demon spirits. The Bible calls these the "vain repetitions" of heathen prayers.

Our prayers are too often like that—closer to witchcraft than worshipful reliance on God. Usually, we're doing our own thing, our own way, on our own timetable. Then when we get stuck, we hold a "prayer meeting" to say some magic words over our problems. Finally, we hope that the God who designed and created the universe will intervene and bless our petty agendas.

Many times, our loving heavenly Father does grant some of these requests, but leanness comes to our souls. We end up missing the intimacy and joy we would have experienced by waiting on Him to learn His will. And, of course, we cannot go on adding the phrase "in Jesus' name" to our wish lists forever without inviting chastisement from the Lord.

God has promised to honor the prayers spoken in Jesus' name only when they are just that—requests which come out of our spiritual intimacy with Christ. Such intercessions qualify to be in His name only because we are in Christ.

Sadly, by taking certain scriptures out of context, some Bible teachers have distorted the concept of prayer for many in our day. Prayer is not a "free ticket" to health, wealth and prosperity as these "witch doctors in disguise" would have us believe.

Chapter 16

The World, the Flesh, the Devil

Prayer is not a new product to be marketed. Today we have prayer towers, prayer cloths, dial-a-prayer, live prayer lines, books, prayer letters, tapes, maps, diaries, prayer clocks, beads, charms and trinkets galore—but less real prayer than ever. There are endless seminars, workshops, retreats, and courses on prayer. But the question must always be asked, Where is the living God in the midst of these products and events?

It is not mere instruction and seminars that we need. Instead we need men and women who will get on their knees and pray. Those who will do this, depending totally on the living God, are the ones God will use to shake this generation. In his book *Why Revival Tarries*, Leonard Ravenhill cries out for reality in this critical area:

"No man is greater than his prayer life. The pastor who is not praying is playing; the people who are not praying are straying. The pulpit can be a shop window to display one's talents; the prayer closet allows no showing off.

"Poverty-stricken as the church is today in many things, she is most stricken here, in the place of prayer. We have many organizers, but few agonizers; many players and payers, few pray-ers; many singers, few clingers; lots of pastors, few wrestlers; many fears, few tears; much fashion, little passion; many interferers, few intercessors; many writers, but few fighters. Failing here, we fail everywhere.

"We ... mistake action for unction, commotion for creation, and rattles for revivals."

Too often, we equate learning about prayer with the real thing. For others, the promotion of prayer has eliminated prayer itself. What passes for prayer in these cases is more often the mindless activism that mistakes motion for life.

Prayer is not a management technique. The Christian calendar is crowded with so-called prayer meetings, 24-hour prayer chains, marches, vigils, nights-of-prayer, half-nights of prayer and a host of other prayer movements covertly designed to promote secondary causes.

Some of these are real. Others are merely used as a promotion technique by religious movements, sects and organizations.

Real prayer is spiritual warfare. It requires us to wrestle with the world, the flesh and the devil—overcoming in the power of His Spirit rather than in our own flesh and mind.

Therefore, the first requirement in prayer is that we come close to God. The more we sit at His feet and look into His eyes, the more our prayers will reflect His mind. Thus, the more we become like Him—the more reality there will be in our prayer lives. We must start to love the people and things He loves—and hate what He hates. As we go deeper into the heart of Jesus, we will pray according to His will because we will know His will.

How can we begin to cross this vital bridge to reality? How can we have a meaningful prayer life?

First, prayer must become priority one. Prayer always comes first in God's timetable. We must reverse the process of modern thinking in order to discover spiritual reality.

In the natural, we begin with our needs and desires—the problems to be solved. We then set goals and plan backwards from them. Rather than waiting on God for direction, we rely on ourselves for solutions. We trust our beauty, finances, intellect, strength and talent. Science and technology have taught us to experiment, study and research solutions.

Those who have bought into this lie believe, if they are given enough time and money, they can solve any problem in their personal lives or in their ministries. Since they really don't believe they need God, prayer plays no part in most of their planning. When it does, it tends to be at the end rather than the beginning of their efforts!

How different this is from the approach of a spiritual man or woman.

The godly person first sets goals on his or her knees rather than at the drawing board. The servant whom God chooses to use is the one who has learned that, if there appears to be any human explanation for our success, it is probably bogus.

This Christian knows that you tend to pray better without computers, degrees, education, money, good looks, management skills or talent. When we are freed from dependence on a human plan, program, leader or other resources, then we are able to trust God rather than ourselves.

Until we learn to lay aside our reliance on every human resource and learn to make waiting on God the number one priority in life, we are still in the kindergarten of prayer.

Second, we must invest time in prayer. Of course, taken by itself, long hours spent in prayer are not a sign of closeness to God. It is more important that we come into His presence, like childless Hannah did, with desperate abandonment and submission to His will. She was speechless before God, and yet the Lord gave her the miracle of conception in answer to her silent pleadings.

However, our time diaries too often betray our callous indifference to God. The simple fact is that no one can get to know God without spending time with Him. If we love the Lord as we say we do, how can we spend so little time in His presence?

We struggle to make quality time for friends and family. Millions of us plan our lives around favorite TV shows, sporting events and vacations. Yet why is it so hard to make an appointment with God—to spend an hour or two each day in prayer?

How many of us can say we spend as much time in prayer as we do in eating meals and socializing around food?

Our lives are so over-booked with frantic activity that we have scheduled Him right out of our days. Is it any wonder our Christianity is so ineffective, weak and powerless? There is only one way to see a change. We have to make prayer a priority and set aside time for it every day.

An Invitation to Every Believer

Christ is calling every believer to come apart and enjoy spiritual intimacy with Him through various aspects of prayer: adoration, confession, intercession, listening, thanksgiving, petition, praise, singing and waiting on Him.

This is not an invitation open only to a few dare-saints—but an access into the presence of God offered to all New Testament believers. And it is all of grace through faith. God wants to have this intimacy with us more than we will ever know.

I received a call once from a lady in California. She was bedridden and couldn't move from the neck down. But she had a world map mounted on her wall. As she lay there, she would pray for seven hours a day. This was her work.

As she told me about the various countries she had been praying for, it was amazing to me to see that these were the very areas in which we've been experiencing open doors and revival.

Prayer works. We as individuals can make prayer a part of our daily lifestyle, if we are willing to break from our culture and live for God.

I know housewives who are able to pray while they do dishes, fold laundry and do other household chores. Others pray and praise as they ride to work. Each of us can rise early or schedule other times to be alone and wait on God.

In early 1976, when the Lord began to break my heart over the lostness of the world, one of the first things we did as a family was to call a few of our friends and start a prayer meeting in our home. That Tuesday night meeting still continues without fail after all these years.

We spend the first part of the evening in worship and praise with brief testimonies and thanksgivings. We don't spend the time chatting but hear reports from different countries of the world, individuals, tribes and unreached people groups. We read prayer letters and requests from all over the United States and Canada as well as overseas. Frequently we will pause to break into small groups or pairs to pray over each request.

In this way, we have seen hundreds and hundreds of specific answers to prayer. If there is not a missions prayer band in your church or neighborhood, why not start one? If one already exists, why not go and add your faith and warmth to that group.

If you would like some tips on how to have a balanced, lively prayer meeting, just write me and ask for a copy of our brochure *Guidelines for Effective Prayer Meetings*. I'll be happy to send it at no charge.

God Delights in the Prayers of His People

Second Chronicles 16:9 reveals the heart of God in this matter: "For the eyes of the Lord run to and fro throughout the whole earth, to shew himself strong in the behalf of them whose heart is perfect toward him. ..." He wants to bless us. He's looking for those with hearts totally after Him.

The world is looking for beautiful, self-confident people to lead and entertain it. But God is looking for humble, Christ-dependent people who will love the world as He does.

For those who are willing to confess their utter dependence on God in prayer, life enters the realm of the supernatural. And this power is available to families, churches and organizations where individuals are willing to start living a prayerful life.

Hebrews 11 and countless other passages reveal to us throughout history that there have always been a handful of people who will reach out and touch God in faith through prayer. As we join them on our knees, we will see the power of God operate in our lives as they did. We will receive the vision and guidance we need to move supernaturally with God and accomplish His will.

Today, there are races, nations and peoples still without Christ. There are families breaking up all around us and individuals caught in sin. There are prisoners who need to be freed, hungry who need to be fed and sick who need to be healed. There are churches and neighborhoods and individuals in your own community which need a touch from God. The Lord is looking for individuals who are emptied of self-sufficiency to accept prayerfully the challenge of reaching those lost billions with salvation. Through prayer you can intervene in these needy lives and situations—bringing the power of God into the lives of the lost and lonely.

Won't you, through times of personal and corporate prayer, join in the cosmic struggle to win them to Christ?

Chapter 17

God Has Blessed America

God wants to speak to you in the everyday events of your life if you will only open yourself up to Him. Let me illustrate with a true story taken from a page of our family album.

My son, Daniel, is a gymnast. This means we as a family often are called upon to support him and his team at their gymnastics meets. As I was in the midst of writing this chapter, I drove the whole family down to San Antonio, Texas, one Saturday for an invitational meet.

There God spoke to me in a special way about His love for America and the plan He has for this nation—if we will only walk in obedience to Him.

As nearly 100 young athletes gathered to start the competition, we stood solemnly with all the other parents for the national anthem. My wife, Gisela, remains a German citizen, and I am a citizen of the country of India. (This way we have greater access to mission fields.) But our children, born in the United States, are citizens of this great country.

My eyes turned automatically upward to the huge American flag that hung at one end of the brilliantly lit hall. Then God spoke to me as "The Star-Spangled Banner" played. I felt an overwhelming rush in my spirit from God. I realized that I was looking at the flag of a nation unlike any other on earth.

My mind flashed back to the past 14 years since I landed on the soil of this wonderful country. I recalled the day I arrived in the Dallas airport with $8 in my pocket and a few clothes. I didn't know anyone. The school where I was enrolled made known my situation to other students. Richard Shaffer, a Pennsylvania native, came and picked me up and took me to his house. For the next six months or so, I stayed with him. He loved me and took care of me as if I were his own brother. Everywhere I went, I saw love and acceptance. I was amazed, knowing that I was a stranger, and they didn't have to go out of their way to show kindness and love to me.

Moreover, what other nation, I asked myself, would have helped us to establish a house and a mission organization? Who would have let us send out millions of dollars to preach the Gospel to people whom they have never met? I have traveled to scores of nations but never have been to a country where people are so open and gracious as in the United States of America.

As these thoughts filtered through my mind, my eyes were misty—and a voice from the depths of my heart rose like a voice of an orchestra with a thousand voices, saying, "Lord, thank You so much for America. Thank You for Your kindness to me and to my family in bringing us to this country. I pray that You will continue to show Your kindness to this nation, that once again, O Lord, this nation will be a nation called by Your Name, and a people who truly fear the living God." Once again, I pledged to pray for America more than ever.

Of course, we have problems here in this nation. I don't deny that. But take any problem you have here and multiply it a thousand times, and you will begin to understand the problems other nations experience around the world. Don't misunderstand me—I am not trying to water down the sin and lukewarm Christianity we find today. Those to whom much is given, much shall be required, and I know God is beginning to ask an account for all the blessings He has given us in this nation.

As you read this book, I share my heartfelt sorrow for my brothers and sisters in this nation. I don't speak as one who is condemning, but as a family member, talking to you out of love and concern. We must not be satisfied by comparing ourselves with our neighbors, but we must compare our lives, where we are, with the high calling of God given to us. We must be willing to repent, get up and press forward for greater things in the days to come.

The United States is a peculiarly blessed country. The Lord God has singled out this land from all others to receive His special favor. Few nations in the history of mankind have had over 200 years unbroken by foreign invasion, poverty and plague. Never has any people enjoyed such freedom, peace and prosperity.

God Is Speaking to America Today

This present generation of Americans, in particular, is receiving the most unearned and undeserved favor of all time. God has made this people the richest nation on earth, yet Americans carry on as if this wealth were a natural right—as if they have no obligation to a lost world, dying in darkness without Christ.

God has been so patient with us. Why this awesome grace continues must be a question all heaven asks! Surely the United States today deserves His judgment and punishment. Yet the Lord has continued to show mercy to these wayward descendants of the Mayflower and Jamestown believers. The living God has been keeping the covenants those first settlers made with Him, mercifully keeping His promises to a prodigal people.

In my last meeting with Leonard Ravenhill, we discussed the mystery and wonder of God's long-suffering love for the American people—and the fact that it cannot go on much longer. I'll never forget his chilling words: "It's coming. If God does not judge this nation, He'll have to apologize a thousand times over to Sodom and Gomorrah."

May God teach us that all these blessings are only temporary and conditional. May He help us to see how late the hour is and how urgent it is we respond with obedience to His grace and mercy.

Jesus said the fields are white unto harvest now. Anyone who has worked on a farm knows what that means. When you've got a ripe crop in the field, everything else stops. You harvest it or it rots in the ground.

God has prospered us for a purpose. He is the king of Matthew 25:14-30 who entrusts wealth to his servants and goes on a long journey. When he returns, the king demands an accounting and a profit from what he has given to invest. What will we present to our Lord when He returns for an accounting? What kind of stewards are we being with the blessings He has shed on this nation?

A People of Privilege

North Americans don't know what an unbelievable privilege it is to be born or to live in the United States or Canada. I could write volumes about the abundance of education, food, health care and housing in the West. There's nothing a person needs here that isn't inexpensive and plentiful. Even homeless street people in the United States live infinitely better than many in poor nations.

While much of the Asian world works from dawn to dusk for a few handfuls of rice, many Americans are more concerned with how to lose weight! While many people in the world can't read or write, Americans worry about choosing the "right" school for their children. While much of the world barely has two changes of clothes, many Americans are concerned primarily with the latest fashion and color.

I don't really need to develop this point. Most North Americans are already vaguely aware of these material luxuries and privileges, although they rarely pause to thank God for them. But we seem to be less aware of the spiritual luxuries we enjoy. Let us concentrate on this area for a moment.

First of all, in the United States, we know about Jesus. Even if His beautiful name is used as a curse word or joke, virtually every American has at least heard the Christmas story. Most have heard the Gospel repeatedly. How different this is from my native Asia.

For nearly six years I wandered from village to village and street to street in north India as a native missionary evangelist. Everywhere I would ask the same question, "Have you heard of Jesus?"

I cannot tell you how many times we would hear the reply, "Sir, there is no Jesus Christ living here. Maybe he lives in the next village. Why don't you try there?"

Millions of people in Asia have not once heard the Gospel, have never seen a Bible, a tract or a Christian video. Hundreds of millions have never heard a Christian radio broadcast or even met a believer—let alone spoken with a trained missionary evangelist.

Hundreds of thousands of villages are without a Christian witness, and there are 11,000 unreached people groups in the world still without a church! Most of these are in Asia.

Many times, when I quote these gigantic numbers to audiences, I see eyes glaze over. These numbers have been heard so many times they have lost their impact. But remember, we're talking about real people with lost souls. These are not monkeys jumping up and down, or fish in the sea, but people who are born and die, love and hate. They suffer loneliness, guilt and pain just as you and I do.

May God open our eyes to the reality of the nearly three billion people who are still unreached by the Gospel of Jesus Christ. As our global population exceeds six billion people, we face a situation where there are more people living on earth today than have lived in the whole history of humankind.

Compare this crying need overseas to the present situation in the United States alone:

• More than 1.5 million Americans are ordained ministers, leaving about one preacher for every 187 persons.

• There are more than 600,000 churches, 6,100 Christian bookstores and over 4,000 Christian radio and television stations. Also, we have countless Christian schools, colleges and seminaries.

• More than 95 percent of the total church budget in the United States is spent at home to maintain programs rather than to reach out in mission. Of the five percent that goes overseas to mission, less than half of one percent is used to reach the lost.

• Only one percent of overseas North American missionaries is concentrating on going to the unreached people.

To understand this inequity fully, imagine the 55,000 seats in the Houston Astrodome represented the population of the world. If 171 hot-dog vendors represented all the missionaries we send overseas, 170 of them would be offering food to only the first 25,300 seats. One lone vendor would have to go to the other 29,700 seats!

And it's worse than that. When they had gone through those first 25,300 seats once, they wouldn't go on to the other rows full of hungry fans! Instead they would go back over the first seats again and again and again. That's what is really happening in Christian missions today.

And the situation here at home is the worst scandal of all. A tiny slice of the world's population, living in the United States and Canada, is getting stuffed with the Gospel over and over again while most of the world is still waiting for a first bite.

Although only eight percent of the world's population speaks English, more than 90 percent of all Christian ministry is conducted in the English language. There are over 4,300 language groups in the world which still do not have a Bible translated into their own tongue!

Our first reaction, I suppose, should be to fall on our knees and thank God for the privilege of living in a nation that is super-saturated with the Gospel. But next, we need to ask ourselves seriously why God has given the United States these tremendous material and spiritual resources.

Chapter 18

Call to Missions

The Bible teaches in Luke 12:48 that with every privilege is a corresponding duty. "For unto whomsoever much is given, of him shall be much required. ..." Surely God has not permitted Americans to be the richest people on earth by chance.

As Christians, how can we not use our position of privilege and wealth to advance the kingdom and win the world to Christ? The acid test of our commitment to Christ is the depth of our involvement in what concerns Him the most—world evangelization.

How can we say He is Lord unless we are seeking to fulfill the greatest longing of His life—to carry out His orders and finish the task He began on the shores of Galilee?

Jesus said in Mark 16:15 that we are to go to the "whole world" with the Gospel. It would appear some people think this means just to people of their race who live on the right side of town. Others with a really "big vision" seem to think it means the United States. But Jesus gave a clear command. We must have a world vision that reaches to our own "Jerusalem" as well as our "Judea, Samaria and unto the uttermost parts of the earth."

The benchmark of your love of God is your burden and committed action for the whole world—not just your part of it.

What clever, spiritual-sounding excuses I've heard in my travels.

One of the most interesting excuses blames God for our problems. It usually begins with, "But, Brother K.P., you don't know my ..." and ends with a sob story about some old defeat, hurt, sin or temptation. I call this the "wounded soldier" excuse.

With love in my heart, the only thing I can say to this excuse-maker is, "I understand. But no matter how badly you've been hurt, you're in a million times better shape than any lost sinner walking down the road to hell. If you think you've got problems, how would you like to worship a demon god that demanded you sacrifice your newborn baby by cutting her throat before an idol? How would you like to worship a god that demanded you throw yourself alive into the flames of your husband's funeral pyre? Or how would you like to be enslaved to a religion that forced you to bow down and worship the rats that were eating your grain and causing your children to starve to death?"

It's all happening in Asia today and around the world—wherever people are enslaved to heathen religions.

Another excuse that has a nice ring to it goes something like this, "Brother K.P., what about my _____?" You can fill in the blank yourself: career, children, church, education, health, insurance, family, retirement. This excuse is based on the idea that God does not love us and will not provide for us if we serve Him.

There are as many other excuses as there are people, but one of these days each of us will have to stand alone before God and repeat them if we dare.

Your children. Your boss. Your parents. Your pastor. Your spouse. Your friends. None of them will be there with you then. All the people you've tried to impress with your spirituality or sophistication over the years will not be there. You will stand alone and look into the eyes of Jesus. You will have to answer to God for what you did about the lost world.

In Ephesians 2, Paul describes the unredeemed as living for the things of this world and the flesh. Instead, the chief characteristic of our lives is to be that we "seek those things which are above." (Colossians 3:1)

Why not stop this minute and take a spiritual inventory of your life? Are you living for eternal realities, or is your life centered around getting more of the things of this world or protecting what you already have?

When was the last time you laid aside your shopping list, your problems, your needs, your family and said, "Here am I, Lord, send me!"

Spiritual reality always burns with a compelling, driving purpose. Christ has given us as individuals and as a nation the most exciting task imaginable—to be the bearers of His love and salvation to a world lost in sin and darkness.

Into the Heart of Jesus

The heart of the Lord I love beats for the lost. From Genesis to Revelation, the Bible is one long love story. Until we as believers can enter into that love, we don't have the strength to pick up our cross and follow Him.

Does this kind of passionate commitment to world evangelism seem unreal to you? Do you not yet weep over lost souls and nations without the knowledge of God? Do immorality and sin no longer affront your sensibilities?

Is all this talk about world evangelism and the kingdom out of touch with your everyday life and concerns?

Are you able to pray for your own salvation, for your family and loved ones—but not for the lost millions of this needy world?

May I then challenge you to pray a simple little prayer that has changed my life forever? I believe it can do for you what it did for me late in 1976.

I'm not sure where I read it, but one day I came across a little anecdote in a booklet. A certain preacher was in a dry spell. The spiritual fire had gone out inside. His heart no longer beat with a love for the lost.

In desperation, he fell on his knees and cried out to God, "Please stamp eternity into both of my eyes!"

When I read that, I knelt right then and prayed the very same prayer with all my heart. What a change it has made.

Take your present age and add 100 years to it. Where are you now? Where is your car? Your house? Your library? Your furniture? Your clothes? Where are all the things you worry about—and pray for—and save for—where are they now?

Measured against eternity—nothing of this world makes much difference at all. A hundred years from now, it is unlikely that even one person in the world will remember what we looked like in this life!

But heaven is real. Hell is real. This is what gave Jesus such purpose and urgency in His ministry. Jesus knew the reality of eternal death where lost souls tumble year after year—forever—into a fiery bottomless pit where the flame is not quenched and the worm dieth not.

This is why He could stand and weep over Jerusalem. This is why He kept pressing on relentlessly from one village to the next. This is why He became homeless, hungry, faced danger and rejection. It is why He finally chose to go voluntarily to the cross. This is why He left us with His Great Commission.

You see, Jesus lived with eternity in view. He had come from eternity, and He was going back to eternity. He never was out of touch with spiritual reality. No wonder He could live a life for others as a selfless servant.

Jesus knew that He was "the way, the truth, and the life: no man cometh unto the Father but by me." Yes, our Lord knew there is a heaven and there is a hell. He knew that He was the only way to get to heaven and not go to hell. That's why He loved lost souls so desperately and was willing to spend His ministry reaching out to sinners of all kinds—bigots, drunks and prostitutes, as well as respectable religious folks who were just as lost as the rest.

Many times I have struggled with this fact: Jesus is the only way to God—and without Him, lost sinners will spend forever in hell. I have wished it weren't so, but it is so. Jesus taught it, and that fact sent Him to the cross. Jesus was gripped by a passionate love for the lost, and we need to let ourselves be consumed by the same spiritual reality.

This is the only way we can enter into the reality of His life of love. We have to see the lost world as Jesus sees it. How can we be the body of Christ if we're not thinking as He thinks, loving as He loves and being motivated by the things that motivate Him?

In my first book, *Revolution in World Missions*, I told about my life-changing meeting with Bob Pierce in Singapore. I'll never forget the tears in his eyes as he prayed, "Lord, break my heart *again* with the things that break Your heart."

On the road to spiritual reality, we must come to that point where we can see the lost world as Jesus does, when our hearts are broken with the concerns that break His.

The Two-Way Test of Maturity

When we learn to see the situation of this lost and dying world as the Lord Jesus does, I believe we must ask two questions about everything we do:

First, *does this fulfill the Great Commission?*

Second, *will this help bring His kingdom?*

If you can say yes to both these questions, then you can be almost certain your next move is the right one. These two questions can and must be asked of every activity, purchase or relationship. This is also the acid test of any corporate decision at your church or in any Christian mission—does this new program or purchase square up? Or is it a tangent that takes us away from world evangelism and building the kingdom?

When my wife and I first returned to the reality of this kind of kingdom living back in 1976, I remember even praying about getting a $2 haircut, because in those days that $2 bought 1,000 Gospel tracts. I believe every detail of our lives should be lovingly and prayerfully measured against this yardstick. And I'm not advocating legalism. This is the simple obedience that any love-slave joyfully owes his master! Too many today misunderstand obedience as legalism, just as they confuse knowledge with action.

Jesus makes no apology for demanding obedience in this area. If you're not putting the kingdom first, how can you be on the road to spiritual reality? You are either in sin and need to repent—or you're kidding yourself about being a born-again Christian. The word "Christian" means "little Christ"—how can we truly follow Him when we're in direct disobedience to His most basic demands?

Chapter 19

The Army of God

The Great Commission sums up the mission of every individual Christian and every church and every Christian organization. It is the standing orders for the army of God. It is the Lord Jesus Christ's last and final charge to us before He ascended to the Father.

Jesus, when listing the signs of His second coming in Mark 13, said, "And the gospel must first be published among all nations." Through the centuries many have believed this to mean that Christ will not return until the Gospel is preached to every tribe and tongue, and at this moment there are still 11,000 people groups without a Gospel witness!

Could it be that the only reason Christ has not returned for His bride, the church, is our failure to fulfill the job description He left behind for us?

The actual words of the Great Commission are repeated five times in the New Testament, once in each of the four Gospels and once in the book of Acts. In each version, there is a slightly different emphasis. If you've not already done so, commit it to memory in each of the five records. Here is how they are translated in the King James Version:

Matthew 28:18-20: *"All power is given unto me in heaven and in earth. Go ye therefore, and teach all nations, baptizing them in the name of the Father, and of the Son, and of the Holy Ghost: Teaching them to observe all things whatsoever I have commanded you: and, lo, I am with you alway, even unto the end of the world."*

Mark 16:15-18: *"Go ye into all the world, and preach the gospel to every creature. He that believeth and is baptized shall be saved; but he that believeth not shall be damned. And these signs shall follow them that believe; In my name shall they cast out devils; they shall speak with new tongues; They shall take up serpents; and if they drink any deadly thing, it shall not hurt them; they shall lay hands on the sick, and they shall recover."*

Luke 24:46-49: *"Thus it is written, and thus it behoved Christ to suffer, and to rise from the dead the third day: And that repentance and remission of sins should be preached in his name among all nations, beginning at Jerusalem. And ye are witnesses of these things. And, behold, I send the promise of my Father upon you: but tarry ye in the city of Jerusalem, until ye be endued with power from on high."*

John 20:21-23: *"Peace be unto you: as my Father hath sent me, even so send I you. And when he had said this, he breathed on them, and saith unto them, Receive ye the Holy Ghost: Whose soever sins ye remit, they are remitted unto them; and whose soever sins ye retain, they are retained."*

Acts 1:8: *"But ye shall receive power, after that the Holy Ghost is come upon you; and ye shall be witnesses unto me both in Jerusalem, and in all Judaea, and in Samaria, and unto the uttermost part of the earth."*

The Lord Jesus never intended us to go out in our own strength. He promised miraculous power and authority to those who would wait on Him. These verses hint at nothing of defeat, self effort or human weakness.

The Great Commission passages leave us no option. They present an unmistakable mission statement to every believer and to the church. The first task of every Christian is to extend the Gospel to every *people-group* on earth. Anything and everything else must be subordinated to this great work.

That means every activity, every building, every effort, every program, every organization and every project are to be evaluated in terms of how they contribute to the ultimate mission of the church—world evangelization in our generation.

Understanding the Kingdom Principle

The supreme importance of the Great Commission in Scripture raises troubling questions from sincere believers who are really seeking the will of God. Many come to me with troubled questions about how to prioritize the Great Commission and integrate it into the rest of their lives.

Does it mean that every believer should be a full-time foreign missionary? How do we relate the Great Commission to the other commands of Scripture? What about church programs to feed the hungry, heal the sick and house the homeless? How do we relate the crying demands of the unfinished missionary task to family and our everyday life and work?

I am so grateful to God for the loving counsel and direction that my dear friend David Mains, of the Chapel of the Air, has given in this matter. Through David, my eyes were opened to see the divine balance that Christ taught in these matters.

That's why we need to ask the second test question of every decision we make about time and money: Is this really helping to build up the kingdom of God?

As we fully understand the Great Commission and the principles of the kingdom together, we will find that they are one unbroken piece of cloth, a single weaving.

I believe that 2 Corinthians 5:14-21 teaches us that we are all Christ's ambassadors, sent to represent Him to the lost and dying world around us. Verse 18 says He has given us the ministry of reconciliation to bring our neighbors back to God. And in this work of reconciliation, we all are assigned different places in the harvest field. But there is only one harvest and one master of the harvest. We need to work together and support one another in the common task.

Love Should Rule

It's as if we're building a house. One person builds doors, another builds windows and another works on the roof—but we're all building the same house. It doesn't really matter who is doing what task so long as the house gets built.

Love should rule among the workers, but one of the saddest things I find today is that many don't understand this principle. Satan has deceived some into thinking that only they are building the kingdom. So they end up fighting mad, convinced that they can't work with others who don't look exactly like them, act exactly like them, and believe exactly the same way.

Of course, I'm not talking about compromising basic Christian doctrine. We can never work with those who are not united with us on the essentials, but those seldom divide Christians today. We are mostly divided around pet doctrines, methods, personalities and structures. Too often, we're building our kingdoms instead of His kingdom—and that is just plain sin.

Once we understand that we have only one king and we're building only one kingdom, we should be able to start praying and working with everyone. There's no other way we can reach a world which has a population of more than six billion souls.

So, while every Christian is required to be a witness in his locality and sphere of influence—one must also become a "sender" of missionaries simultaneously. Not many Americans will actually have the privilege of going with the Gospel to an unreached people group. But we all can help while we attend to whatever the Lord has called us to do in the kingdom.

We need to see this principle, and when we have, it is the most liberating revelation. No longer do we have to protect our association, denomination, ministry, race or vocational calling from other Christians. In my native tongue we have a little proverb which goes, "It doesn't matter who pounds the rice so long as it gets milled." That's how we should view others in the kingdom, supporting them as much as we can as each does his or her part to finish the task before night falls.

Unity in Christ

It's when we realize this fact of the unity we have in Christ that the great growth really begins in our spiritual lives. When we stop fighting one another, we are free to act on the really important questions:

How do we extend the rule of Christ in our chosen career—to our boss, co-workers, competitors and peers?

How do we extend the rule of Christ in the lives of our spouse and children and parents?

How do we help extend the rule of Christ into the realms controlled by principalities, powers and authorities—some of which might even be governing our lives and ministries?

This is why the New Testament so often describes our pilgrimage on this earth as warfare or an athletic contest. The Christian life is to be a gentle life of loving our enemies, but we can never for a minute forget it is not a life without terrible enemies. We are called to a life of conflict and confrontation. But it must be with the real enemies, not with fellow believers.

Can you see why "self" must be on the cross for us to have victory in this spiritual warfare? If ever we try to build a personal kingdom rather than His kingdom, He cannot support us in the battle. If ever we want *our way* instead of *His way*, then the game is lost.

This is one of the biggest reasons why so many Christians find themselves defeated—even in church work and ministries that outwardly appear to be good and righteous in themselves. It is why we find backbiting, envy, jealousy and lust surfacing even in the best churches, Christian organizations and families.

Plainly, however, this is not necessary. How? In the next chapter I have some suggestions.

Chapter 20

Get Involved Personally

Paul reveals the secret to indifference in Romans 15:20 where he says that he strived to preach the Gospel "not where Christ was named." We should learn to be on the lookout for opportunities to share Christ with those who haven't had a chance to hear—wherever they may be.

There are three basic ways that you can get involved in world evangelism:

First, become an informed intercessor. There are all kinds of resources available to help you learn more about missions and pray for frontline outreach.

Read up-to-date books on what's happening in the world of missions today, such as *Operation World* from OMLit, *On the Crest of the Wave* from Regal, and *Revolution in World Missions* from GFA Books.

Hang national and world maps of various mission fields in your home, office and church facilities. There are many excellent sources for these maps. Some also include beautiful illustrations of various "ethno-linguistic" people groups, national backgrounds and names of leaders. The "Operation World" Prayer Map from OMLit is one of the most popular. Of course, you can also order secular maps from the National Geographic Society and cartographers.

When God touched my family with a renewed burden for lost and dying souls, one of the first things we did was hang a big map of Asia in our kitchen with pictures of native missionaries nearby. Our children are growing up praying for and learning about the lost world.

Subscribe to missionary magazines, newspapers and prayer letters. Literally thousands of such periodicals are published by denominations, missions and Christian organizations. One of the most helpful tools is the *Global Prayer Digest*, which provides daily prayer updates on the progress of world evangelism.

Go on a vision tour to the mission field. Many missions sponsor tours of Buddhist, communist, Hindu and Muslim nations. If such a visit is well-organized, you can see firsthand the sacrifice and service of front line native missionaries. For many, even a week or two in a closed nation can be a life-changing experience.

One warning, however: two weeks or two months on the mission field does not make you a missionary! It takes a lot more than a brief visit and some volunteer work to disciple new believers and plant churches. We have found vision tours to be one of the most life-transforming experiences possible if they are organized properly.

Second, become a faithful prayer warrior. There are all kinds of ways you can remember front line Gospel workers in prayer.

Spend time alone every day remembering the needs of native missionaries, sending organizations and the unreached peoples.

As you read newspapers, watch television and absorb other media, send out sentence prayers for people and places you learn about.

Work with your pastor, Sunday school leadership and other church organizations to see that prayer for missionaries is included as a regular part of all worship and group activities.

Third, get involved personally. You can become a world Christian. There is something for everyone to do.

Help sponsor a missionary yourself. For as little as $1 a day, you can help support a native missionary working in the remote areas of Asia.

Work to get others to become sponsors. Prayerfully share the vision for the unreached peoples and native missionaries with your pastor, group or class leaders. Often the group can make world evangelism a line item in its budget and sponsor a native missionary. At other times, you may get permission to challenge others to become missionary sponsors. Many sending missions have films, speakers and videos available to help you tell the story of various missions to your church or small groups.

Go to the mission field as a short-term volunteer. Many times there are behind-the-scenes ways you can become a servant to native missionaries and churches in the Third World. In some areas, short-term volunteers can be effective in literature distribution and evangelism. I thank God for ministries like Operation Mobilization and Youth With a Mission, which are helping hundreds of young Americans spend two years in overseas service. I believe God wants to send forth tens of thousands more from these shores—even if it is only for one or two years. I am convinced that there is a place for learners and servant-hearted young people in the Third World mission fields.

Evangelize representatives of unreached peoples in your community. Many students and visitors from closed countries are short-term visitors to the United States. These include Arabs, Buddhists, Israelis, Hindus, Marxists, Muslims and many others from nations where the Gospel is suppressed. Your friendship, hospitality, prayer and witness to these could help introduce them to Christ. Historically, such contacts have helped win whole nations and states to the Lord.

Help arrange for a missionary conference at your church, or better yet, a united annual festival of missions for your whole community. Volunteer to serve on the missions committee of your church. There are many resources available from various missions and associations to help you arrange such events.

Finally, you can go as a missionary yourself. I believe there are a few people reading this book whom God is calling to go "to the uttermost parts." Others may think that you are throwing your life away, but if you obey, God will open doors to places where you can be effective and used of Him on the front line.

How long has it been since you've gotten down on your knees and prayed the prayer that Jesus must have prayed every day, "Lord, please use me to reach the lost—not my will, but Thine be done"? There is something He would have you do. You can play a part in this great end-time drama. Don't let anything stand in the way of giving your best for the cause of Christ.

World Evangelism Now Possible

We are on the verge right now of the greatest explosion of evangelism in history.

God is doing a miracle today in world missions. Throughout the Third World, He is raising up tens of thousands of native evangelists and church planters who speak the language and understand the culture of the people they are called to reach. This new soul-winning army is already on the move, going to their own people with the good news of redemption in Christ.

These native missionaries are incredibly effective. In Thailand, for example, where 150 years of Western missionary efforts have yielded only a handful of believers, recent efforts by native missionary teams are resulting in thousands coming to Christ every month. One native missionary evangelist has alone led 10,000 people to Christ using simple flip charts. Another, committed to disciple-making according to 2 Timothy 2:2, has seen 12 generations of converts develop from the first one he led to Christ.

Those are the kind of miracles we're seeing today, not only in Thailand but in India, Myanmar, the Himalayas and the Philippines.

Finishing the task of world evangelization in our generation has never been more possible than right at this moment. African leader Gottfried Mensah, former executive director of the Lausanne Committee on World Evangelization, has made what Ralph Winter calls "an electrifying, simple proposal." He says that if we were to let every 1,000 evangelical believers in the world today select and support one missionary couple from their midst, and send that couple to one of the 11,000 hidden people groups, every tribe, tongue and culture would have a missionary witness.

Reaching the 500,000 villages of India could easily be done if just one out of every 92 evangelicals in America sponsored a native missionary. That's less than one percent of the evangelicals in the United States—and it would be enough to support 500,000 full-time pioneer missionaries in India!

Opportunities Are Many and Great

It can be done, and by God's grace it must be done.

At this moment, thousands of native missionaries are ready to go to the unreached if only support were available. The nation of India is the greatest open door in the world for missions at this time. The need there is outstripped only by the opportunity. Similar situations exist in nearby lands such as Myanmar, Thailand and the Philippines.

But what is actually happening now on the American scene? What are Christians in the United States doing to respond?

I read a little article in the *Indian Express* that said the United States is now sending more money to India to support Hinduism than for any other cause. Christian missions was rated much lower on the list as number seven of all the foreign exchange earners between the United States and India.

Every villager in India, even where they cannot read or write, knows what Coca Cola is! Marketing firms like Avon cosmetics have more than 1.4 million sales people worldwide peddling soap and makeup. That's 21 times more than the total   number of missionaries America sends to the whole world! Mormonism, a false cult, is able to field 30,000 young missionaries every year—four times more than the total number of evangelical missionaries doing pioneer evangelism worldwide.

What a rebuke these figures are to the disobedience and rebellion of so many Christians and churches today. Our Lord has given us the command to go, the spiritual power to go and the material resources to go. How much longer will we continue to be the bottleneck that prevents world evangelism?

We need to rediscover the purpose for our lives. As I was writing this chapter, a top computer programmer from a Fortune 500 company came to me to talk about Christian service.

He had been working for this company for 17 years and was making a salary that was comparable to $100,000 in today's economy. But he was miserable with his life and work.

"All I do," he said, "is write programs, train people to run them and write more programs. I want to use my skills and training for God."

Praise the Lord, he is now serving in a Christian organization.

God is not calling all of us to leave our jobs and go into full-time Christian service as this brother and his wife are doing. Others need to stay and develop their careers and vocations—but find ways to send more of their earnings to the mission field. Still others can give volunteer work to help spread the vision for missions in the churches of the West. I believe that God has something special for each of us to do in this great work of world evangelism.

There is no longer any excuse for us to live mediocre, washed-up lives without a sense of purpose and mission. Every Christian has something to do in this great task of world evangelization.

Chapter 21

Loving Is Sharing

The streets of India—especially in our bloated, over-populated cities like Bombay and Calcutta—are maddening to Western visitors. Millions of homeless people are born, live and die in them. Part toilet, part barnyard, part roadway—they are also the bedroom, living room and marketplace for the poorest of the world's poor.

In summertime's furnace heat, the dust of centuries rises from them to fill your eyes, choking your mouth and nose. In the monsoon rains, the streets turn into vast seas of mud and sewage. In winter, the freezing pavements bring disease and death to those who have nowhere else to rest their starving bodies.

It was on one of these nightmarish streets of Bombay that I was surrounded by an army of begging children. Already late and on my way to an important meeting, I tried to ignore the pleading children as I waited for the light to turn green.

Suddenly from the sea of hungry faces I heard a voice so distinct from the rest that I was paralyzed. In crystal clear tones I heard her speaking in plaintive Hindi, "Sir, my father died three months ago of tuberculosis. My mother is too sick to beg anymore. My little brothers and sisters have not eaten for two days. Please, sir, they are hungry and crying. Can you please give me a few pennies so I can buy some bread?"

The light turned green. But I couldn't move. I was arrested by the image of this little girl who must have been about 9 years old. Her face was one of the most beautiful I've ever seen, perfectly shaped with big brown eyes and long black hair.

Through the tears on her cheeks, the dust and the sweat, I could see that in different circumstances this desperate little waif could easily have been a princess. Her filthy hair had obviously not been washed or combed for weeks. She was barefoot and dressed in rags. But I'm still sure she had the potential of being a winner in the Miss World beauty pageant.

Jesus Loves All the Children

Then something else happened. It was as if another face came before my eyes right beside hers. It was another child, about 8, also with big brown eyes. But she had long, clean hair and a shining face. Her clothes were fresh and colorful—and she wore nice socks and tennis shoes. I knew her. She was the best student in her class. Each night she said her prayers and read the Bible. Her parents loved her. She had a comfortable home, air-conditioned from the Texas summer and heated in the cold winter. She had a comfortable bed with clean sheets every week. I didn't know the name of the dirty little beggar girl, but I did know the name of the girl beside her. It was Sarah, my own darling daughter.

Then I heard a supernatural voice beside me ask, "What is the value of this beggar girl? Is she of less value than your daughter, Sarah?"

I knew the answer from the Bible. Instinctively, I answered, "No, Lord—Jesus loves all the children of the world."

But even as I replied, I realized that God was not asking me the question I had answered. He was asking me something more personal and life-shaking. He was really asking me about my priorities. Was I willing to love this beggar girl as Jesus loved her—in the same way that I loved myself and my own wife and my children? Would I love her with real love, the kind that shares?

You see, God is asking us to focus on the principle of love. This is the only force powerful enough to propel us across the bridges of detachment and simplicity. Only love can draw us to reality in our handling of material things, and only love can prevent us from shipwrecking on the rocks of legalism in this critical area of spiritual discipline.

The Law of Love

When Jesus was challenged to name the greatest commandment and thus sum up the moral teaching of the Old Testament Torah, He quickly answered His accusers, "Thou shalt love the Lord thy God with all thy heart, and with all thy soul, and with all thy mind. This is the first and great commandment. And the second is like unto it, *Thou shalt love thy neighbour as thyself.*" (Matthew 22:37-39, emphasis mine)

This is the hinge upon which all Christian outreach turns. This is what most truly motivates us to become agents for redemption in our Jerusalem, Judea, Samaria and the uttermost parts.

I read the sad story of a father in Waco, Texas. His son had been diagnosed as having cancer and needing life-saving treatment. The frantic father sold the family house, car and pickup truck to pay medical bills. When these were gone, a garage sale dispersed of everything else—even their clothes. When there was nothing left to sell, he borrowed all he could. But in the end the boy died.

How much was that boy's life worth to the father? It was obviously worth *every*thing and *any*thing. That's how we love when disaster hits our own lives or the dear ones we love in our own families.

How Much Is a Soul Worth?

What are your own life and comfort worth to you? You find out when you get even a little toothache or headache! You run to the medicine cabinet. You go to the drug store. You go to the doctor. You pray for healing.

How much is your own eternal soul worth to you? Probably quite a lot or you wouldn't be reading this book. It's the reason why most of us come to Christ and go to church. We realized that our sin was taking us to hell, and that's why we repented and called on God to save us. We care about ourselves. We want to spend eternity in heaven with our Lord and Master.

We want the same for our children, our parents, our spouse. You see, we love our own souls, and we love the souls of our dear ones. We don't want them burning eternally in the flames of hell, separated from God and falling into the bottomless pit forever and ever. So we agonize over them and share Christ every chance we get.

This is what God is saying to us. If the very thought of one of our loved ones living on the streets of Bombay breaks us up—and if the thought of a dear one in hell is unthinkable—then how can we say we love our neighbors and let them go on an express train to hell?

Walkers—Not Just Talkers

What about the millions who are desperately waiting and wanting to hear the Gospel in Myanmar, India, Thailand and the Philippines? What about the other millions who are being denied the Gospel in the Maldives, Nepal, Tibet, Turkey and North Vietnam?

Whose responsibility is it that native missionaries are sent into these nations now occupied and ruled by the forces of darkness? If the affluent and wealthy Christians of the West will not share with the lost, who else on this earth can afford to send forth the laborers?

We have thousands of missionaries waiting now to go to lost tribes and hidden villages—but 96 percent of all the Christian resources are being spent in America to reach just six percent of the world's population. While millions of Christians in other nations still don't have a personal Bible, many in this country have several copies—often bound in luxurious leather, which costs 30 to 40 times more than a simple Asian Bible.

Where does real love fit into all this—the kind of love that shares? When they asked Jesus essentially the same question, He told the story of the Good Samaritan who stopped and helped a stranger in need. I like the force of James' teaching on this subject in chapter 2, verses 15 and 16: "If a brother or sister be naked, and destitute of daily food, and one of you say unto them, Depart in peace, be ye warmed and filled; notwithstanding ye give them not those things which are needful to the body; what doth it profit?"

James says God wants walkers, not just talkers. In 1 John 3:16-18, the Bible says, "Hereby perceive we the love of God, because he laid down his life for us: and we ought to lay down our lives for the brethren. But whoso hath this world's good, and seeth his brother have need, and shutteth up his bowels of compassion from him, how dwelleth the love of God in him? *My little children, let us not love in word, neither in tongue; but in deed and in truth.*" (emphasis mine)

Caring is sharing. Loving is sharing. Missions is sharing. The whole purpose of the church in this world can be summed up in that one word: sharing. That is what the agape love of the New Testament is really all about. It is what the Great Commission itself is all about.

But millions of Christians are still in spiritual kindergarten because we have been taught only to acquire and receive rather than practice true *love by sharing.*

Chapter 22

Live as Christ Would Live

In my first book, *Revolution in World Missions*, I related my American experiences from 1974 to 1980.

In 1976, during the darkest times of my soul, I had to learn the reality of detachment and simplicity. Satan had me so pressured with ministry burdens and support problems at one point that I almost gave up the ministry.

One time, the pressure became so great I considered making our lives more bearable by going into real estate, so that we would have enough money to pay bills and ministry expenses and at the same time keep up our present lifestyle. My wife saw what was happening, and she begged me to continue to trust the Lord and live with nothing, rather than to alter God's calling on my life.

I'm so glad I prayed through this hard time, and God gave us liberty and freedom to learn to seek His kingdom first and to trust Him to meet our needs. We learned to alter our lifestyle, rather than compromise His call.

I'm not sharing this story of our family to lay down rules for you. God assigns each of us to a different place in the harvest field, and thus we must answer to the Holy Spirit in our own way as to how we handle finances and material things. This is simply how it happened at our house.

You and your family will have to find your own road to detachment and simplicity. It may be quite different from ours, and that's fine. I hope only that our story will illustrate basic principles and give you some direction for your journey into this area of spiritual reality.

Brainwashed by Demons

Our society seems to be pursuing an increasingly materialistic lifestyle, and we as believers are not immune to it. We act out guidelines we receive from Christian and worldly advertisers alike. We aim to live the "good life," as advertised on television and billboards and in the press.

We are brainwashed by the demons that drive American media, and we have it all—or we are on our way to having it all! We have closets full of suits, ties, shirts, dresses, blouses and shoes for every season. We own several cars, a savings account and insurance policies. We have a house and a mortgage to go with it and, of course, credit card debt. The television is always on, and we subscribe to popular magazines and newspapers. We can't live without ice cream in our freezer, and we drink sodas between meals. We eat cakes and cookies and junk food. We wash with perfumed soaps and have a medicine chest full of cosmetics, medicines and spray cans.

I Was Miserable Inside

My family and I were not unaffected by the materialistic lifestyle around us, and we, too, were caught up in this same spirit. On the surface, everything was fine. I was preaching, studying the Word for hours daily and shepherding a flock of 200 souls. Our church was growing. The congregation was being fed the Word of God. People were being saved, but I was miserable inside.

My soul was drying up. I was tormented by the knowledge I carried inside my heart and head. Others had not seen what

I had seen in Asia, and I could not forget the people I had left behind. I was haunted by memories of millions of lost souls in north India, and the suffering, forgotten little band of native missionaries I knew was still trying to reach them for God.

So for two years, my heart had hardened. I had not shed a tear for them. In fact, I could not shed a tear for anyone or anything. Then, as I prayed and evaluated my life in the light of eternity, it all changed. I let go of one materialistic thing after another—to surrender my ambitions and plans for future ministry in the safety and security of America.

During two weeks of prayer, I made a deliberate decision to put it all on the altar and let God once again have total control of my life. Suddenly, a dam of tears broke within, and I could once more weep and feel the love of Christ for lost souls.

My lifestyle was up for grabs. Everything and every action were tested against the literal teaching of Scripture. I decided that I would lay up no treasure for myself on this earth. I made a definite choice to put the kingdom of God first and trust Him to "add all these things unto me."

Our lifestyle became simpler. My new car was the first thing to go. Insurance policies, savings accounts, credit cards, most of my clothes—everything that could be was sold off so the money could be sent to needy native brethren.

But we never missed a thing. It was such a joy to move in the flow of the Holy Spirit again. Suddenly we were free. We had wings like eagles to soar above our bondage to these material playthings. In one stroke, we as a family were again having a significant impact on a lost and dying world. We knew that we were exercising the mind of Christ about these things, and we began trusting our Father to provide for our needs.

A Changed Lifestyle

In fact, finding new ways to save money for missions became a game at our house. I started washing with generic soap instead of fancy brand names. Magazine subscriptions and wasted hours before the television disappeared from our lives as did the time I once spent matching the color combinations of my wardrobe.

I had no regrets. We were no longer seeking to improve our lifestyle, worrying about investment portfolios, saving for a rainy day—and all the other nonsense which cripples and destroys the lives of so many Christians in this country.

May I challenge you, dear reader, to go prayerfully through your house and your life with Jesus at your side. Take along a yellow pad and make a list. Ask Him to speak to you about your garage, basement and overflowing clothes. I challenge you to pledge your allegiance to Him in such a way that you'll surrender anything He asks.

May I dare you also to reverse your prayer-style when it comes to the way you spend your income.

How many Christians pray before they go into the super-market? How many pray before they go to the mall or shopping center? Before they buy a book or a magazine or go to a movie? Before they go to a restaurant where the cost of the check would sponsor a native missionary for a month? How about you?

Yet the minute they are challenged to support the real work of God, things become very spiritual. Now they have to pray about sponsoring a native missionary, pray about responding to appeal letters for missions, pray about contributing to the offering!

I'm not saying we should be careless stewards in how we support missions, but I am saying that most of us apply a double standard which is not based on agape, sharing love. If the spending of our income is for our things and our pleasure, then the signal is "buy—buy—buy!"

But too often, when lost souls are at stake, we let greed and hoarding call the plays. Then we have to think about it and consider it. And we don't do this only in our personal lives. The same kind of thinking prevails when we make corporate decisions at church.

Recently I heard about a church which purchased a $100,000 chandelier! Another church is making a $52,000 weekly mortgage payment! When it comes to approving a ski trip for the youth group or new carpet for the sanctuary, the item passes through the budget committee without comment. But if it is Bibles for Myanmar or supporting a native missionary, then there needs to be debate. This is the opposite of how we should be thinking.

How Jesus Handled Money

Jesus had much to teach about money—how we use it and give it. He also left us a good example of how to handle funds. It is found in John's account of the Last Supper. There the apostle makes a little aside that gives us vast insight into the priorities Jesus used for dispersing funds during His earthly ministry.

Judas, the treasurer, had finished his dialogue with Jesus and was about to leave the table to betray Him. The Lord makes a simple remark that is misunderstood by the other disciples. He says to Judas, "That thou doest, do quickly."

Now how did the others interpret that remark? They had been with Jesus for three and a half years. They knew the job description of Judas—and they had carefully observed how Jesus spent money. So they thought Judas was going to go out and do what he always did. They figured the Lord was sending him out either to buy needed things or give aid to the poor. That was the way Jesus used money, to purchase immediate necessities and help the poor. What an amazing insight into the mind of Christ and one that fits well into all the other teachings of our Lord about the proper use of earthly things.

Everything about Jesus and the apostles reinforces this strong impression. They were frugal men who had learned to master money and use it as a servant of the kingdom rather than as an end in itself.

Our problem today is that we believe all the money that comes to us belongs to us to spend as we please. We have the crazy idea that if God gives us a $100,000 annual income, He wants us to live a $100,000 lifestyle for ourselves.

The apostles knew better. They lived a lifestyle that matched their responsibility to a lost and dying world. It showed in the kind of the churches they planted. The New Testament Christians were living examples of Christ's control over earthly goods.

The most famous example is the Jerusalem church where "all that believed were together, and had all things common; and sold their possessions and goods, and parted them to all men, as every man had need. And they, continuing daily with one accord in the temple, and breaking bread from house to house, did eat their meat with gladness and singleness of heart, praising God, and having favour with all the people. And the Lord added to the church daily such as should be saved." (Acts 2:44-47)

The Principle Applied

Here we see the principle of New Testament sharing applied to the everyday lives of the early Christians. Again in 2 Corinthians 8 and 9, we find a long passage on stewardship principles that repeats the sharing concept: "For ye know the grace of our Lord Jesus Christ, that, though he was rich, yet for your sakes he became poor, that ye through his poverty might become rich. ... For I mean not that other men be eased, and ye burdened: But by an equality, that now at this time your abundance may be a supply for their want, that their abundance also may be a supply for your want: that there may be equality: As it is written, He that had gathered much had nothing over; and he that had gathered little had no lack." (2 Corinthians 8:9,13-15)

According to shocking statistics from the U.S. Center for World Mission, only one-half of one percent of our church budgets in this country is used to preach Christ to the 3.8 billion unreached people of the world. More than 95 percent of our church budgets are spent at home. Of the 5 percent that is sent overseas for missions, 4.5 percent goes for social work and for subsidies to establish churches on the mission field.

Can you imagine what would happen if Christians in the West were to grasp the principle of sharing and apply it to the needs of the Gospel around the world today? Within a few short years, native missionaries would have preached the Gospel in every lost village of the Third World!

Could it be that the worship of money and materialism is at this moment keeping the world in the dark about the good news of salvation?

Here's my challenge to you: *Live on less if that's what it takes— but determine right here and now that you will live as Christ would in your financial affairs.*

I'm convinced that, if we would adapt the kind of radical, sharing lifestyle of the New Testament, we would turn our world upside down for Christ. If we would live according to the economic laws of the kingdom, we would easily be able to send out new missionaries by the hundreds of thousands. In our lifetimes, we would be able to provide the Word of God to every human being on this planet.

And, of course, this powerful economic witness would be felt here at home as well as overseas. As we become detached from our worship of earthly things, we would learn to live more relaxed and contented lives. This freedom from covetousness and greed would allow us to escape the frenzied "earn, spend and consume" syndrome that drives our culture. This is the merry-go-round which Satan now uses to hold our families, churches and society in economic bondage. But this bondage can be broken.

Chapter 23

God and Riches

O ur whole approach to material things should orbit around the extensive teachings of Christ on money and wealth. Three principles for handling our financial affairs are most clear:

First, *we cannot serve God and money at the same time.* In Matthew 6:24, Jesus says, "No man can serve two masters: for either he will hate the one, and love the other; or he will hold to the one, and despise the other. Ye cannot serve God and mammon."

God and riches are mutually exclusive masters. We must choose one or the other.

Money will either be our master or our slave. In Luke 16, we are told God cannot entrust true riches to us unless we have conquered and subdued our natural attraction to the riches of this world—and controlled them for the kingdom. Here we are told we are stewards only. That means we're to administer the possessions of our Master—not even consider the things we own as ours.

Nowhere does the Bible teach we can't earn or have money, but it does teach that we cannot love it. We cannot be friends with it for an instant. We cannot secretly desire the normal extravagance of our worldly neighbors, or we will find ourselves consciously or unconsciously doing things to obtain it. Either we love God or we love money. No middle ground is tolerated.

Watchman Nee, in his book *The Spiritual Man,* emphasizes this truth: "We need to follow our Lord's admonition to remember Lot's wife, for she was one who did not forget her possessions even in a time of the greatest peril. She was not guilty of having retraced a single step toward Sodom. All she did was look back. But how revealing was that backward glance! Does it not speak volumes concerning the condition of her heart?

"It is possible for a believer outwardly to forsake the world and leave everything behind and yet inwardly cling to those very elements he had forsaken for the Lord's sake. It does not require a consecrated person to return to the world or to repossess what he had forsaken in the world to indicate that the soul-life is still active. If he casts one longing glance it is sufficient to disclose to us that he does not truly recognize where the world stands in relation to the cross.

"Gaining spiritual life is conditional on suffering loss. We cannot measure our lives in terms of 'gain;' they must be measured in terms of 'loss.' Our real capacity lies not in how much we retain but in how much has been poured out. Those who can afford to lose the most are those who have the most to give. The power of love is attested by love's sacrifice. If our hearts are not separated from love of the world, our soul life has yet to go through the cross."

Each of us must settle this point once and for all, or we will find it coming up again and again. Throughout our lives, Satan will use it as a lever to weaken and destroy our walk with God. We must not be satisfied until we have internalized a hatred for the true, idolatrous nature of money. The Holy Spirit longs to bring us all to a place where we have no more attraction for it.

Second, we are to lay up treasure in heaven—not on the earth. Matthew 6:19-21 says, "Lay not up for yourselves treasures upon earth, where moth and rust doth corrupt, and where thieves break through and steal: But lay up for yourselves treasures in heaven, where neither moth nor rust doth corrupt, and where thieves do not break through nor steal: For where your treasure is, there will your heart be also."

This passage is not difficult to understand if you simply take it at face value. We are not to store up wealth on this earth and accumulate things down here but invest everything beyond basic necessities in expanding the kingdom of God.

The deepest meaning turns on the definition of treasure.

When does money become a treasure in our lives? When it is $1,000 or $50,000 or a million dollars? Jesus very wisely refused to define an amount or percentage. He did this for a very good reason. I have seen even $1 become a treasure for the poor brother or sister that desires to possess and hold it.

If anything of this world has its grip on us—be it a bank account, securities, retirement plan, car, house or clothes— that is a treasure. We are not to attempt to "possess" it, hoard it or hold it, since nothing of this world is ours to keep.

Everything that comes into our hands belongs to our Lord and Master, Jesus. Thus we must always hold it loosely, willing for Him to ask us for it at any time, investing it gladly in the salvation of souls and the furtherance of the Gospel.

Third, we are not to be anxious or worried about the future. Matthew 6:31-34 says, "Therefore take no thought, saying, What shall we eat? or, What shall we drink? or, Wherewithal shall we be clothed? (For after all these things do the Gentiles seek:) for your heavenly Father knoweth that ye have need of all these things. But seek ye first the kingdom of God, and his righteousness; and all these things shall be added unto you. Take therefore no thought for the morrow: for the morrow shall take thought for the things of itself. Sufficient unto the day is the evil thereof."

How ridiculous for us to plan and pursue riches, saving for "a rainy day" when Christ has promised us that God will supply our every need when the time comes. How many millions of Christian lives are wasted and remain useless for the Master because we are preoccupied with worries about the future?

Detachment in the Old Testament

God has always honored the believer who has learned how to stay detached from the things of this world. The Old Testament is filled with many examples, some positive and some negative, that teach us the importance of nailing our love of material things to the cross.

Job lost everything and was still able to worship God.

"Naked came I out of my mother's womb, and naked shall I return thither: the Lord gave and the Lord hath taken away; blessed be the name of the Lord," he says in Job 1:21. He was tested, as I think we all are in this area—but he was able to say, in effect, "Praise the Lord, I won't be bothered!"

Abraham responded graciously and refused to fight for material advantage.

In Genesis 13 we see a family feud developing over grazing land between Abraham and his nephew, Lot. Money divides families and friends. But Abraham backed off and let Lot have the well-watered plains of Sodom because he wouldn't let riches become an issue. This is the attitude of a godly man, and the Lord blessed him for it. He promised him all the land he could see from Hebron. Lot, meanwhile, lost everything in the end, including his family and wayward children. What a lesson today for those families who have to have two incomes to keep up with the Joneses and are willing to sacrifice the future of their children for material gain.

Balaam sold out his ministry and eventually lost his life.

In Numbers 22 we see the tragic decline and fall of a good prophet who had refused to deal with his attachment to the things of this world. He was only able to resist up to a certain point. When Balak offered a small bribe, he said no. But finally, when the price was too much to resist, he yielded and lost everything. How many still fall for this trap today! If there's money involved, without praying we automatically consider it a blessing, but it can just as often be a test from the Lord or a snare from hell.

Achan wasted the lives of his family and brought defeat to his nation because he lusted after material things.

In Joshua 7, we see how Achan first gazed upon forbidden treasures, then coveted them, took them and finally hid them—all against the commands of God. These are the four inevitable steps to sin in this area of material matters. In the end, we find poor Achan shamefully hiding these spoils. Whenever you have to hide and apologize for your financial affairs or wealth, you know something is desperately wrong.

Gehazi pursued a gift that brought the curse of leprosy upon him.

Here is the sad story of a servant who went after Naaman for a financial gift which the prophet Elisha had already refused. God was doing a spiritual work in the heart and life of Naaman, but Gehazi made the foolish mistake of trying to profit from it. Here is a man we would call a full-time Christian worker today, privileged to serve on staff of a great prophet. Perhaps if he had only been faithful, he would have in turn received a double portion of Elisha's spirit as Elisha had from Elijah. Instead, he and his descendants went to their graves as lepers forever.

Detachment in the New Testament

The rich young ruler left Christ brokenhearted, unwilling to trade wealth for his own soul.

Here was an outwardly perfect young man who kept the law and sincerely appeared to want eternal life. But then Jesus put him to the test. He was told to go and sell all, give to poor and follow Jesus. The request proved too great. He went away sorrowful because he loved and trusted his riches more than God. This prompted Jesus to make a remark that amazed the disciples: "A rich man shall barely enter the kingdom of heaven." They had been raised to believe that riches were a sign of God's favor and blessing, but Jesus identified them as a great hindrance to salvation.

Judas sold Jesus for 30 pieces of silver and ended up a suicide.

Here is a well-educated, religious man who walked and lived with Jesus throughout His earthly ministry. He was patriotic and so well-respected that none of the other disciples ever suspected that he was a traitor. But the Bible tells us that he was a thief who was so enslaved to money he could betray the Son of God for a few coins. Judas undoubtedly knew by heart the teachings of Christ about wealth, and yet when the test came, greed won out.

Ananias and Sapphira lied, holding back part of their offering—and both lost their lives for it.

They thought they were fooling men with the way they handled this pledge, but Peter makes it clear that they were trying to lie against God and the Holy Spirit. We cannot hold back our tithes or fail to keep our vows in matters of finances.

From these examples and the teachings of the New Testament, it is plain to see that even religious, apparently godly people can easily be destroyed by an unsanctified love for earthly things.

Chapter 24

New Testament Simplicity

L earning to use earthly things correctly is one of the great est challenges facing Christians today.

Extremists and false teachers abound, teaching asceticism on one hand and the prosperity gospel on the other. For those seeking reality, we must avoid both extremes and learn the balanced teaching of the Bible on how we are to handle money.

Let's say you knew for certain the future of international relations, and you knew there would be a nuclear war soon. Let's say you also knew the exact targets, and they included your home town, your working place, your house—in other words, everything you have in this world.

How would you live with such a knowledge? Your material things wouldn't mean much to you, would they? Or your career, home, car, art collections or whatever else you now prize. I'm sure you'd want to do everything you could to save your family, friends and loved ones.

Such knowledge would create a radical shift in anyone's priorities. Yet, as Bible-believing Christians, we have just such an urgent knowledge. We know with absolute certainty that everything in this world will soon be completely burned up, and that everyone we know and love will die within a few years. And we know that billions of others around the world also are on their way to an eternity without Christ.

With this knowledge and what the Bible teaches about sharing, love and detachment, just how should we be living?

The conclusion is inescapable: *In light of the present world condition and the commands of Christ, we must give everything above basic necessities to complete world evangelism.*

Each of us is assigned a different place in the harvest field. The meaning of simplicity will therefore vary from time to time and place to place, but no Christian is exempt.

We need to learn to live the lifestyle that we read about in the Bible. In Luke 14:25-35, Jesus is talking about nothing less than a radical life of sacrifice—one where we count the cost and decide that we will pay the price by turning our backs on the luxury lifestyles our culture has conditioned us to expect. "So likewise, whosoever he be of you that forsaketh not all that he hath, he cannot be my disciple." (Luke 14:33)

If you are living for Christ, you don't look at your living room and dream of what kind of furniture you can buy. Instead, you find ways to do without or wait on God to supply.

Paul wrote to young Timothy, "No man that warreth entangleth himself with the affairs of this life; that he may please him who hath chosen him to be a soldier." (2 Timothy 2:4)

We are already at war. The day we acknowledged Christ as our Savior we signed up for battle, and that's why I'm calling on every Christian to start living in the light of spiritual reality.

I'm calling on believers everywhere to join me in a radical, far-out life of simplicity that will seem crazy to many of your family and friends. You can live a greedy, self-indulgent life. Or you can choose the way of the cross, living for others as Jesus did and still calls us to imitate today.

While writing this chapter, I sat down with some friends for an hour of brainstorming. Our goal was to think of as many ways as possible to simplify our lives and save money for world evangelism. We came up with a list of 53 items—none of which was a major sacrifice.

Here are a few of them.

Shoppers

Avoid designer labels and nationally advertised brands. Buy generics and house brands.

Use "cents off" coupons only for the things you normally buy and save them for double and triple value sales.

Buy sale items only when they are already on your shopping list. Plan your purchases using lists and budgets. Buy cheaper toilet paper and paper products.

Pay cash and don't use credit cards or interest-bearing time payment plans.

Wait at least 24 hours before you buy a large ticket item. Don't window shop.

Buy at thrift stores or warehouse/outlets. Buy in bulk instead of small quantities. Buy from friends or garage sales.

Buy used cars and major appliances instead of new.

Don't buy convenience gadgets. Don't buy sports vehicles such as boats or recreational vehicles.

Leave your checkbook at home when shopping and take only the cash you will need.

When buying appliances like telephones, get the inexpensive ones without extra features you rarely use.

Be aware of product cycles and wait to buy at end-of-season and clearance sales.

Finally, eliminate harmful and addictive products from your shopping list.

Parents

Organize a baby-sitting co-op with friends and neighbors; organize car pools to transport children to events.

Be moderate in giving toys to children; become more involved in free outdoor activities.

Use libraries instead of buying books and records; explore

museums and other free activities; bring picnic lunches on outings rather than purchase expensive junk food from concessions and vendors.

Use Sunday comic sections for gift wrap at children's parties. Make church activities the center of your children's social life rather than expensive worldly entertainment.

Give your children time and attention rather than trinkets.

Housekeepers

Make a budget for expenditures and stick to it.

Use water sprays rather than aerosol starches for ironing; learn to eat more rice; cut down on expensive red meats.

Write letters and notes rather than use the phone.

Cut down on use of electricity and other utilities, especially heating and air conditioning.

Use reusable plastic food containers rather than depending on plastic wrap and foil to store leftovers. Instead of letting small bars of soap melt or be thrown away, get them wet and attach to new bars of soap.

Fast regularly.

Make a list of essentials you need to live on and then start eliminating and selling everything else. Wash full loads of laundry and dishes.

Freeze and save leftovers for later use.

Repair things rather than throw them away; do preventive maintenance on your car and house in order to fix things cheaply before they get worse.

Finally, go through your house once a year and have a garage sale of everything you don't need or use.

Employees

Bring your lunch to work rather than eat out to save both time and money.

Shop for clothes that require minimum care and coordinate with existing wardrobe. Wear classic clothes rather than latest fashions.

Buddy-up and share professional resources with others in your chosen career.

Avoid vending machines.

Ladies

Reduce use of cosmetics and beauty products. Avoid seasonal fashion buying; watch out for fad diet products and household gadgets you use once and throw away or store unused in closets and cabinets.

Men

Don't buy hairpieces; wait for sales to buy suits and shoes. Don't purchase rarely used sporting goods such as exercise equipment and firearms. Avoid purchase of professional cameras and video equipment. Carefully evaluate the real need for expensive power tools and elaborate stereo systems.

Everyone

Shop around for haircut prices and go with classic styles rather than fads and fashions.

Cut down on magazine and catalog subscriptions. Buy used quality items rather than cheap new products.

Send notes rather than greeting cards. Evaluate and reduce gift-giving, particularly at Christmas.

Evaluate and reduce cost and length of vacations. Reduce costly entertainment and recreation lifestyles. Avoid fancy restaurants.

Reconsider the cost of keeping and feeding pets. Reconsider costly collections and expensive habits.

Clergy

Reconsider and simplify use of vestments and ecclesiastical furnishings. Reduce the size of your library and don't buy books you will use only once.

Re-evaluate the entire church budget every year to channel funds away from selfish uses and toward missions. Set aside at least five percent of your gross budget for frontline native missions and cut elsewhere in your programs, if necessary, to make sure that this minimum goes overseas.

Re-evaluate the efficiency of your current missionary programs, especially those which support American missionaries or social services. Realize that most mission efforts which rely on American staff—or provide social services—are no longer effective.

Use Material Goods for the Kingdom

Again, let me stress that these are only a few ideas that may or may not apply in your particular situation. All Christians are called upon to find ways to simplify their own lifestyles as the Holy Spirit directs.

The most important goal is to employ material things for the kingdom of God rather than ourselves. This is one of the truest tests of where our affections really lie. Christ demands nothing less than lordship of our whole being, including the material blessings we have accumulated in this life.

It's not how much we give that counts—but how much is still left sticking to our fingers. That is the only way to measure correctly the simplicity of one's life. It remains one of the most private, spiritual self-examinations we are required to make, but absolutely essential if we are to have the spiritual reality we seek.

John Wesley once said, "To lay up treasure on earth is as plainly forbidden by our Master as adultery and murder."

Throughout his long life as a best-selling author and speaker, Wesley, had he lived today, would have been a millionaire many times over. Yet he diligently operated his affairs so that he never had more than a few dollars in his pocket. He conducted a worldwide ministry, yet he always said he handled his financial affairs with such simplicity that there would be no need of a will or executor for his estate.

And he was true to his word. By the time God called him home, friends and family were amazed to find Wesley had indeed quietly and systematically given it all away to the Lord's work. Nothing was left but the loose change in his pockets.

Chapter 25

God Wants You

God is in no trouble. He does not need our service, time or talent. To think He does after one has heard the call of God often leads many young believers into wasted years of fruitless labor.

In 1976, when God called me back into missions from the pastorate, one of my first excuses for not moving ahead in obedience was my pulpit. After all, I argued, this church is obviously being blessed, and "God needs me here."

How foolish! We have to learn that God doesn't need us anywhere. He is not helpless!

Regrettably, today too few volunteers are ready to do the work of the Gospel. Almost every day we have a missionary conference on how to win the world to Christ—but the work remains undone because we don't have men and women with servant-hearts who will go out and lose their personal identities in getting the work done.

Unless we are willing to see ourselves unknown, unrecognized and working behind the scenes, there is no hope for our spiritual service ever to bear real fruit in the economy of God. This is the main reason why I believe God is no longer pleased with many of the denominations, missions and Christian organizations today.

That is also why it is so important we enter into the servant-heart of Jesus. The Jesus-style is the servant-style, and it is the only acceptable approach to Christian service.

Jesus said that "the Son of man came not to be ministered unto, but to minister." (Matthew 20:28) And we are to "let this mind be in you, which was also in Christ Jesus." (Philippians 2:5)

Individual believers, Christian churches and missions that refuse to recognize servanthood are traitors to the cause of Christ and do untold harm. Sadly, there are many Christians in our day for whom the New Testament concept of servanthood remains a mystery, "And whosoever will be chief among you, let him be your servant." (Matthew 20:27)

Education, family background, talent, beauty, voice, riches and intelligence mean absolutely nothing to God. He doesn't need our abilities any more than He needs our money.

How sad it is that many talented believers go along for years looking good on the outside, but remaining absolutely useless to the Lord. It is quite possible to be doing the Lord's work and still not to have entered into servanthood. And so enormous efforts, studies, plans and labor are extended— all uselessly because they cannot stand up to the fires of judgment.

How tragic! And what a contrast from the Spirit-filled service of a surrendered Christian servant. When you really commit yourself to God, He commits Himself to you. Lives are changed. Souls are saved. People are healed in body and spirit. God gives fruit, and the fruit remains.

A great need exists today for believers who will cease chasing their own ambitions, dreams and plans. God is searching for the man or woman who will wait and ask questions like, What do You want me to do? Where do You want me to do it? When do You want me to do it? How do You want me to do it?

Job Description for Servanthood

Often in his writings, the apostle Paul outlines his job description for servanthood: "Paul, a servant of Jesus Christ, called to be an apostle, separated unto the gospel of God."

The Greek word here for servant is *doulos* or "bondslave." Now a bondslave is no ordinary servant. There is a huge difference.

An ordinary servant is free. He or she is an employee who checks in at 9 a.m. and out again at 5 p.m. The boss has nothing to say about how this servant spends his or her off-duty hours or salary or what the employee eats or wears. An employer/employee relationship leaves the servant free to marry, choose friends and lead a private life.

The bondslave is a different story. This is the slave described in Deuteronomy 15:16,17 who loves his master so much he chooses voluntary, life-long slavery. He has entered into a contract with the master, symbolized in a ceremony during which the servant's ear was pierced.

This kind of servant wants to be a slave. A bondslave has given up future ambitions, family, fortune and personal plans. He has chosen to become property of another. His life is no longer his own.

By the piercing of the ear, the bondslave is saying to the whole world, "I want to stay with this master forever. My ear is open only to him. I give up all my days and all my nights—my hope of family, mate and money. I will exist to do his will."

The ordinary employee has rights. The slave has not. We need to understand that we who belong to Christ have been called to be His slaves, and we no longer have any rights over our lives. Rarely is it necessary to pump up and motivate such people with applause, awards, prizes or salary.

The Christian who has accepted servanthood as normative has turned over himself or herself to the Lord and says only, "Here am I; send me."

I keep a little anonymous poem in my Bible that says it so well. This is the kind of servant spirit that God is looking for today.

> I am seeking for one who will wait and watch,
>   for My beckoning hand—My eye.
> Who will work in My manner the work I give,
>   and the work I give not—pass by.
> And oh the joy that is brought to Me,
>   when one such as this I find.
> A man who will do all My will,
>   who is set to study his Master's mind.

This is what God is calling His people to embrace in these end times—a life of servanthood. He is challenging us to join the fraternity of the involved, a fellowship of believers who realize *the only real truth is truth lived out.*

We can go to conferences, buy tapes, listen to music, read books, attend church services—but see no change. What will it take? How can we move from being the best informed Christians in the world to a life of active service? When will our lives begin to conform to what we know and believe? How can we get to that place where we'll launch out into action instead of mere talk about the lost and suffering millions around us?

The answer is simple. You need to go to the spiritual door-post of your house and lay your ear against the wood. You need to hand the awl to Jesus and say, "Please, Master, pierce my ear. I want to be Your slave forever!"

There can be no change until we change our attitude from that of the hireling to become bondslaves.

We have to give up our imaginations. We have dreamed up the idea that we can have a conditional employment contract with God. The Bible offers no such thing. We must give up the carefully crafted escape hatches we have designed. Voluntarily we must turn our backs on our excuses for disobedience. Only when we realize that Christ asks for nothing less than uncon-ditional servanthood will we begin to walk in spiritual reality.

Christ is not looking today for cheerleaders, but for athletes who will get into the game and play.

Everywhere I go I find people who will gladly sing about missions, study about missions and even pray about missions. But where are the ones with the servant spirit who will get involved with their whole lives? These are the ones who are willing to go, send and suffer to obey the commands of the Master.

Paul mentions in Romans 1:1 that he is separated unto the service of the Gospel. The Great Commission involves *coming* as well as *going*. You cannot go into all the world unless first you have come away from it and separated yourself to follow Jesus Christ. Bondslavery, like marriage, implies total loyalty to the Master. And there is no way we can have this unless we are committed to living a life of separation from all other masters and all other things.

Be Separated From Sin

You cannot serve sin and Christ at the same time. Romans 6 warns that we are not to let sin reign in our bodies.

"Know ye not, that to whom ye yield yourselves servants to obey, his servants ye are to whom ye obey; whether of sin unto death, or of obedience unto righteousness?" (Romans 6:16)

Three of the most powerful words of warning in the Bible are found in Luke 17:32: "Remember Lot's wife." Here is a woman who looked back longingly after the sin and rebellion of Sodom, and it cost her everything.

We can't be looking back to our days of sin—playing games with the lusts of our flesh—and still hope to serve Christ effectively. No, we must hate sin as Christ did, enough to die for it.

We need to picture ourselves crucified with Christ.

Imagine yourself hanging on your own cross of execution. Is there any attraction to sin and the world left in you? Do the temporary pleasures of this world still have an appeal now? This is the death to sin that every servant of the most high God must taste daily.

"But God forbid," wrote Paul in Galatians 6:14, "that I should glory, save in the cross of our Lord Jesus Christ, by whom the world is crucified unto me, and I unto the world."

Be Separated From the World

The Bible says that we cannot love God and the world simultaneously. There is no middle ground. You must love one and hate the other—the Lord permits no other position.

From earliest childhood, we learn the ways of this world. Unconsciously, worldliness entered our minds. But we must unlearn these methods and techniques, becoming like children again if we want to be effective servants in the kingdom of God.

We must learn it is impossible to mix worldly and spiritual methods without hindering the cause of Christ.

Be Separated From the Devil

The Bible teaches that Satan is the ruler of this world, and we see that he rules it with cunning efficiency. It is organized and submitted to a dictator who rules ruthlessly.

In business, education, law, government, media and medicine—even in children's games, fashion, music and entertainment—Satan has established systems to ensnare and enslave the minds and souls of mankind.

We must learn to resist the fiery darts of the wicked one and overcome this evil triad if we want to be servants of Christ. The world, the flesh and the devil are real forces. We must choose to separate ourselves consciously from them.

Sadly, many millions of Christians today cannot follow Christ into a life of servanthood because they haven't made this conscious choice.

I'm not talking about moving our evangelical churches and homes to the suburbs. This isn't biblical separation at all. We're only doing this to avoid confronting the poor, the needy and those enslaved to sin. We're frightened to go where Satan manifests his reign over this world. In many cases we're afraid because in our hearts we know we're not living a totally separated Christian life. And because of that, we still feel vulnerable to Satan.

Jesus wasn't afraid to visit with corrupt politicians, prostitutes and Mafia-types because He loved people who were in bondage to liquor, sin and vice. He deliberately reached out to the underprivileged, sick and poor people of His day.

The true servant of Christ realizes obedience will often be dangerous, risky and unpleasant. It may mean leaving the comfortable little retreats we have built—our homes and churches in the suburbs—to go into the mean streets of the inner city. It may involve leaving our familiar circle of friends to reach out to neighbors with problems, troubled teenagers, the sick and the imprisoned.

Being a servant of Christ also means being involved in some way with Third World missions to the same kind of people— only worse off because they are in places where the Gospel has not even been preached yet. As the great British athlete-turned-missionary C.T. Studd put it, "Some want to live within the sound of church or chapel bell. I want to run a rescue shop within a yard of hell."

Bought With a Price

Servanthood is the normal Christian life. This is not a life reserved only for clergy, missionaries or super-saints. The Lord Jesus has every right to expect each of us to fully abandon our lives to Him. The Apostle Paul tells why.

In I Corinthians 6:19,20 and again in 7:21-23, Paul writes that our bodies and spirits have been bought by Jesus Christ for a price. His blood shed on Calvary has purchased our redemption. Now we belong to Him.

Servanthood is only giving back to God what already is His.

Imagine a situation where a guest in your home steals your wallet. Later, he feels guilty, confesses the sin and returns your wallet. Has the thief done anything wonderful? No, he has only given you back what is already yours. That's exactly how it is when we accept servanthood as a way of life. We are only returning what belongs to Him. We're only doing what we should have done the very minute we were born again.

As a matter of fact, you may have been a better servant in the early days of your salvation experience than you are today. The spiritual temperature in many of our churches is so low right now that a new believer has to become a backslider to feel at home.

If this sounds extreme to you, perhaps you should re-examine your Christian experience to see if you're really saved. I'm writing this message to truly born-again Christians, since they are the ones who must come to grips with the terms of real Christian servanthood.

I am boldly demanding you choose a life of total surrender because this is the New Testament standard for Christian living.

And something else. Blood-bought servanthood is also the only acceptable motivation for Christian service.

If the driving force for your Christian service is anything like adventure, companionship, ego-gratification or power-lust, then it is unacceptable to our Lord. That doesn't mean we quit serving when we detect false motivation. Rather it means we repent of the sin and do the work of God with the right motivation.

If the men and women of this world can die for such petty causes as political independence, material wealth and territorial gain—isn't true servanthood the minimal response we can offer to the love of our Creator? He is, after all, the living God with whom we will spend all eternity. And He has made it clear that servanthood is what He expects from us.

Why Heaven Is a Happy Place

Heaven is a happy, restful, perfect place because only God's will is done there. The angels are not running around in a frenzy trying to change the universe and save the world! No, they wait for orders. The angels understand their servant role.

When we as believers can come to that place in our lives, then we'll begin to understand a little of what it is like to have a servant-attitude. Then God can really use us.

Jesus was a carpenter. That means He made yokes, the wooden collars that are used to hitch oxen to wagons. They must have been very good, very comfortable ones because Jesus said, "Come unto me, all ye that labour and are heavy laden, and I will give you rest. Take my yoke upon you, and learn of me; for I am meek and lowly in heart: and ye shall find rest unto your souls. For my yoke is easy, and my burden is light." (Matthew 11:28-30)

How different this sounds from the frenzied, overburdened lives of so many Christians today!

How we need to learn the meaning of Hebrews 4:9,10, "There remaineth therefore a rest to the people of God. For he that is entered into his rest, he also hath ceased from his own works."

God wants us to lay aside our plans, schedules, schemes and visions and learn to serve Him in the power of the Holy Spirit. He wants to carry us along in our service—to rely on Him for mercy and grace in our times of need.

When you're doing His work this way, there is no need for fights and squabbles, murmuring, complaining and backbiting. We are no longer intimidated by people or circumstances. We are not on a roller coaster of emotions at each victory or defeat, because God is totally in charge. We know all things work together for good because we are called according to His purpose, and we are conducting our work according to His will.

What a glorious relief. What a change from the yokes fashioned by men, organizations, society and the world around us! What a change from the yokes we fashion for ourselves. They are always tiresome, painful and hard to bear.

The most joyful element of entering into servanthood is the relief it brings from the fears, worries and trials that come from projects undertaken in fleshly wisdom and strength.

Chapter 26

The Model of Servanthood

Jesus is the perfect teacher. He called His disciples to follow Him, not to a set of doctrines or a religion. They learned the Christian life by being with Him, submitting to His example and lifestyle—not in the classroom.

He never expects of us today what He hasn't already demonstrated in the days of His flesh. Christ is the ideal example of servanthood. He is, in fact, the suffering servant Isaiah predicted would come to be the Savior of the world in his prophecy 650 years before Christ was born.

First, Christ submitted His will to the Father. He perfectly reflected the will of the Father. So much so that Jesus even declared that, if they wanted to see the Father, all they had to do was look at Him.

On the night before His betrayal, He prayed in the garden, "O my Father, if it be possible, let this cup pass from me: nevertheless not as I will, but as thou wilt." (Matthew 26:39)

In Philippians 2:7,8 we read that He "made himself of no reputation, and took upon him the form of a servant, and was

made in the likeness of men: And being found in fashion as a
man, he humbled himself, and became obedient unto death,
even the death of the cross."

Second, He waited for God's timing and permission. Jesus
always did and said only what the Father commanded.
Throughout His earthly ministry we find Jesus pausing to seek
direction and permission to proceed, even when He knew the
will of God.

At the marriage in Cana, when His mother asked for the
miracle of turning water into wine, He said, "Woman, what
have I to do with thee? mine hour is not yet come." (John 2:4)
Later, when bombarded with requests for a miracle at the death
of Lazarus, I believe that Jesus paused to pray and ask the
Father for the right timing. Then, when God the Father gave
the green light—and only then—did Jesus proceed with the
required miracle.

Third, He deliberately chose the lowest position of servanthood. In John 13 we find Jesus dramatically washing the feet
of the disciples—the very lowest of the lowest jobs which
servants performed in New Testament times. In this single act,
Jesus demonstrated the role He expects of all Christians
throughout all time.

After wiping their feet with His own garment, and thus
making Himself a doormat to His followers, Jesus asked them
if they understood the meaning of His action.

"Ye call me Master and Lord: and ye say well; for so I am. If
I then, your Lord and Master, have washed your feet; ye also
ought to wash one another's feet." (John 13:13,14)

What is the least and lowest service you can find to perform?
What is the most despised thing that needs to be done in your
church, family or group? What needs to be done for missions
in your church and community? If you will identify that task
and perform it, you are moving in the spirit of service that
Jesus demands.

Christian leadership and service are not hierarchical, even
though many of our current organizations are organized along

worldly lines of power. The kingdom is not patterned after corporate America or the military. Instead, it is a fellowship of servants in which we are to let the servant-mindset of Christ become our mind.

Why is this so difficult for us today? What has happened to cause us to lose the servanting style of Jesus in so much of what we do? I think I have the answer.

You Become What You Worship

Jesus told the Samaritan woman at the well that God seeks people to worship Him in spirit and in truth. It is vital that we worship the true Jesus—not just Jesus as Savior but Jesus as Lord. So many only know half of Jesus, the Savior side alone. They've forgotten the Bible never asks us to accept Him as Savior but as Lord.

You see, the Bible teaches us that we become like the object of our worship. I will never forget doing evangelistic work in a village where the people worshipped a snake god.

The people acted like snakes. And they treated us like snakes would—responding to the Gospel team with blind fear and hostility.

This is true wherever you find idolatry. People who worship money and power become greedy dictators. But people who worship Jesus, the suffering servant, will be conformed to His image.

So those who have not developed a life of worship in spirit and in truth have begun a vicious cycle in their spiritual lives. I believe the reason so many have lost their ability to serve the Lord God is simply a lack of worship.

We don't worship because we don't know how to wait.

And we don't wait because we're not slaves.

And we're not slaves because we haven't given up our egos.

And we haven't given up our egos because we won't worship.

Thus we are back to where we started. Worship is the hardest discipline for most of us because it requires us to give up self and take on humility. Many people go weeks without any meaningful worship of this kind—privately or in church.

Ask yourself, When was the last time I was so lost in worship I fell prostrate in humility before Him? When was the last time I was so emptied of self I was speechless before His presence—that I became oblivious to those around me?

I believe servanthood begins right here. Only when we have surrendered everything to Him, when we find ourselves lost in love and worship, can we begin to trust Him with our lives.

He is seeking true worshippers who will come to Him in spirit. He is not looking for wheelers-dealers, negotiators, pledgers or petitioners—but worshippers who have abandoned their plans and prayer lists before coming to the throne of God.

I have found that only in this kind of prayer can we find the love of God which will enable us to abandon everything to Him, including our fears of servanthood. Only in the ecstasy of such worship can we find release from the anxieties, reservations and sorrows that hold us back.

Worshipping in spirit, we can look into the loving and all-powerful eyes of Jesus. When we do that, something wonderful changes inside. Once we have seen Jesus, how can we have anything but trust in the goodness of God to care for His servant—no matter what trials we might be facing in the flesh? Only in such worship does the abandonment of self and the embracing of servanthood become joyful. This is the secret of the New Testament church. How else can we explain the ability of its members to praise and believe God, even as they were suffering for the name of Jesus?

I have discovered in my own life that on my knees before my Master I am no longer a preacher or a missions executive. All positions and titles are irrelevant. Degrees, education and earthly honors mean nothing. Pride is impossible. It is so easy then to give up my own rights and plans. Whatever He asks me to do, be it simply to serve a cup of tea or open a whole nation for the Gospel, I see it all as equal. It is no longer important what He asks me to do—the only thing that matters is that He has asked for it. The Master beckons, and the servant obeys without asking why.

Rewards don't count either when you're really at the feet of Jesus.

It no longer seems important who went into the field first, who worked the longest, who bore the heat of the day. The Master said go, and the Master determines the wages. That alone is enough to satisfy the heart and mind of any true servant.

And, of course, it doesn't matter who gets the credit or what title one has. The true servant would not rob God of any honor. We take no glory for ourselves, remembering always that "we preach not ourselves, but Christ Jesus the Lord; and ourselves your servants for Jesus' sake." (2 Corinthians 4:5)

The High Cost of Servanthood

Jesus warned, however, that this life of servanthood is not lived without cost. He said, "The servant is not greater than his lord" (John 13:16), and, if they persecuted and hated Him, we can expect no better treatment.

In 2 Timothy 3:12 Paul wrote, "All that will live godly in Christ Jesus shall suffer persecution," so this is also the cost we as servants must be willing to pay.

This is so difficult for us to accept in our world of man-pleasing, "I'm OK, you're OK" Christianity. No one wants to be disliked, hated or misunderstood—especially by family, friends and loved ones. But this is often exactly the price to be paid by anyone seriously wanting to follow Jesus into a life of servanthood.

The only way to walk as a true servant is to decide right at the beginning to accept being a nobody like Christ, making yourself of no reputation. You must decide it isn't going to matter to you what people think or say about your lifestyle. You're going to obey Christ whatever the cost, and so the matter is settled.

God may ask you to throw away your future, give up your education and career, abandon your business and inheritance, leave family and friends. He may ask you to drive an old car, wear out-of-fashion clothes from a swap shop, give up romance and plans for marriage, go to the foreign mission field, or move into an inner city slum. And, of course, He may ask you to stay just where you are and live a life of sacrifice, service and witness among your own people. For many, staying home may be harder than going.

But whatever He asks, you can be certain one of your biggest challenges will be dealing with the problems of rejection and acceptance from your peers.

Many will think you're crazy. Often they may be people whose respect and love you want to keep. Sometimes even trusted Christians and clergy will turn on you. But you must obey the Master, remembering the question Jesus asked, "How can ye believe, which receive honour one of another?" (John 5:44)

Today, God is calling out an army of Americans who will feel His heartbeat and accept the call to live a life of radical Christian servanthood. The temptation is to dialogue with the world, seeking understanding, acceptance and sympathy.

But in most cases this only delays the inevitable. Worldly Christians and unsaved friends simply cannot understand. When the Lord calls you away from this mess of lukewarm, half-hearted, plastic-living Christianity, you can be sure many will say you are an idiot. And it does seem crazy to them. We simply must accept such persecution as a normal part of serving the Lord.

Earthly Honor—A Lifelong Battle

This battle against our self-serving desire for glory and honor never ends. The world and even the church continually tempt us to exchange the servant's towel for an earthly reward.

Paul kept the right balance. In 1 Corinthians 4:12,13, he says, "Being reviled, we bless; being persecuted, we suffer it: Being defamed, we entreat: we are made as the filth of the world, and are the offscouring of all things unto this day." In other words, Paul seems to accept and encourage the notion his normal lot is to be the scum of the earth.

But no one, no matter how long in Christian service, is immune to the temptation to seek position and receive honor.

Even the Christian media today often measures the work of God in worldly terms, with an emphasis on big numbers, buildings and programs. Celebrity converts, preachers and musicians are promoted and glorified on Christian broadcasts as if they were movie stars.

While writing this chapter, I received a call from a nationally known pastor. He asked if he could travel with me to India. He wanted to meet some of the frontline soldiers of the cross and was planning to support several hundred through our sponsorship program.

I was delighted to help set up three meetings where he could meet unsupported native missionaries face to face. We chose some of the most unreached areas of India for the meetings, including one in Udaipur, Rajasthan.

There, 250 village evangelists from four Hindu states of north India gathered for three days of conference. Many of the brothers were first-generation believers who came to the Lord from out of a tribal background. Most had walked for hours or ridden bullock carts to bus and train depots.

They were men of the soil, uneducated and without the manners of urban life. They wore wrap-around skirts, open sandals and village homespun. Their feet were dusty and dirty from days of travel. Their skin was cracked and blistered from travel.

But their suffering and pain were forgotten for three days as this famous and successful American pastor opened the Word of God. On the last day, before the men started to return to their villages, he did an unheard-of thing in India. He announced from the platform that the Lord had laid on his heart to wash the feet of all 250 Gospel workers!

Our native leaders looked at each other in shock, shaking their heads. No one could believe this was really happening. No guest speaker from America had ever done this before. But the visitor insisted, saying it was his privilege. He wanted to wash the feet and pray for these men who were going to take the good news of salvation to lost millions.

A big tub of water was carried in, and for the next two-and-a-half hours, this elderly American minister sat cross-legged on the ground and washed the feet of every missionary.

During the whole time, the tent was filled with songs of worship and praise, turning the meeting into a powerful time of revival. Hearts were melted, and the preaching of the Word was engraved into the hearts of all who attended.

For three hours following the service, the native brothers continued to embrace one another, pledging to support each other until death. The leaders were especially moved by the example of a successful American pastor's willingness to serve the suffering pioneer evangelists of the Third World.

"He has stolen their hearts," said one leader solemnly. I realized then the awesome power of servant-leadership in a whole new way.

God is calling every Christian to learn the secret of bondslave service to a world in need—not just in the emotions of a conference but for a lifetime of humble, behind-the-scenes service to the body of Christ.

Part III

A ROLE MODEL FOR OUR TIMES

On the road to Damascus
Saul of Tarsus began a life
which opened the door from
the Gentile world to untold riches
of life with the great Creator-God of
Abraham, Isaac and Jacob.
And this life can be ours.

Chapter 27

Paul, A Dangerous Man

If you are anything like me, by the time you have read these last chapters, you might feel like giving up!

Even as I was writing the chapters, I often felt discouraged. More than once I asked myself, Why should I write this? Is it possible for anyone to live up to it? In the light of the spiritual realities I am writing about, my own heart was also exposed. I realize how frequently I have failed, and still fail, to walk the paths of reality.

Such feelings are not unique. Throughout the ages, many believers have become discouraged after seeing the challenge and the cost of following Christ. Some even have reverted into legalism or started living a double life.

In his book *No Turning Back*, George Verwer says, "Discouragement is one of the most subtle and tricky techniques in the devil's arsenal for stopping the forward movement of the Gospel."

Jesus had to deal with some of these feelings in the hearts of His disciples. In Matthew 19, after He explained the hardships of entering the kingdom of God, the disciples asked, "Who then shall be saved?" In other words, they were saying something like this: "It looks like an impossible task to follow

You and do Your will in this kingdom of Yours. If those who are educated, powerful and wealthy cannot get in and be a part of it, then how can we poor folks ever make it?"

Peter, like the rest, must have felt like giving up and going back to his old business. Indeed, at one point after the crucifixion, he did return to his boat. But, of course, Jesus answers us, "With men this is impossible; but with God all things are possible." (Matthew 19:26)

The question each of us must answer is this: "Would *God ask us to be someone or do something He knows is impossible for us to do?*" Of course not.

In Psalm 103:14, we read, "For he knoweth our frame; he remembereth that we are dust." God knows we are only made of dust. It is extremely important for us to remember this. Out of the dust of the earth God formed us and breathed into us the breath of life. As long as we live, there is always going to be that pull of dust that wants to bring us down and limit us to finite things of this earth. However, it is the desire of the Holy Spirit who dwells in us to give us strength continually, so we will be drawn to "those things which are above." (see Colossians 3:1-3)

So while it is impossible for any one of us to live a life of reality in the energy and the strength of our flesh, with God it is possible for us to live and do the works which He asks us to do. "I can do all things through Christ which strengtheneth me." (Philippians 4:13)

All Power Is Given Unto Him

Earlier we considered the kind of life God wants us to live now. As Jesus Christ was once bodily in the world, so are we now. This is the reality by which we must live and operate.

Jesus said, "As my Father hath sent me, even so send I you." (John 20:21) Again and again we read through the New Testament that those who follow the Lord Jesus Christ are to be the living Christ to a lost and dying world—manifesting the life of Christ in and through themselves. We are to be demonstrating His authority as His ambassadors in this world. It is easy for us to throw up our hands and say, "It is impossible to live a life like that. I am not Christ. I cannot live it. I have tried and tried. It is useless."

When we listen to that demonic voice, discouragement sets in. We lose faith, and soon we find ourselves fighting a losing battle.

We must always remember that as followers of Christ, we are living in a world whose prince still is Satan. We are behind enemy lines. We're like paratroopers who have been dropped into enemy territory. Never forget that we are fighting this spiritual battle in the enemy's camp. Unless you recognize this fact, you will continue to be discouraged, and Satan will push you to the sidelines.

I encourage you rather to meditate on all the resources and the power the Lord has given to us. Let us never forget that, as He gave us the Great Commission, He also promised, "Lo, I am with you alway, even unto the end of the world." (Matthew 28:20)

We are not alone. We are not powerless. We have supernatural strength and miracle power to fight this battle. Instead of listening to satanic propaganda, let's turn to the many promises and encouragements that Jesus has given us in His Word, the Bible. Here we can find examples of godly men and women who have gone before us and triumphed in Christ.

Paul—A Man Like Us

I believe this is one reason why God called Paul the way He did. The Holy Spirit has given us an inspired New Testament example of victorious spiritual reality in the life of Paul. He was an ordinary person, yet we know that in the power of Christ he lived an incredible life.

Here was a man of dust who faced the same trials and temptations we do, yet he fulfilled God's plan for his life. I believe God is telling us through Paul that spiritual reality is possible for every man, woman, boy and girl today. As we understand the principles and give ourselves to this work as Paul did, we too will accomplish the task in our generation.

There is no room for discouragement, but only for encouragement as we see this reality.

Wherever Paul went, people could not forget the impact he made upon their lives and community. He was not like a modern evangelist who has three-point sermons and jokes.

In Thessalonica, the unbelievers testified, saying, "Here comes a man who has turned the world upside down."

In Ephesus, the enemies of the cross, those who hated everything Paul preached, confessed, "Throughout all Asia, this Paul hath persuaded and turned away much people, saying that they be no gods, which are made with hands. ..." (Acts 19:26)

In other words, wherever he went, whether people liked him or not, one thing they could not deny was that this man, Paul, was dangerous. His very presence brought changes in their thinking and living.

We read in Acts 19:13-16 how the sons of Sceva tried to cast out demons from those who had them, and a particular demon spoke back to them, saying, "Jesus I know, and Paul I know; but who are ye?" The demons jumped on those boys, and they fled naked! This tells us that the hosts of hell, the demons, trembled at the very word "Paul." Heaven recognized Paul.

The whole thing boils down to this: Paul lived such a life that he was filled with spiritual authority. He truly followed in the footsteps of his Master.

Mark 13:34 shows the relationship Jesus has with such followers. It is like a wealthy millionaire who has gone on vacation, leaving his estate and power of attorney with his staff. He has left his authority to his servants, just as God has now entrusted His authority to us.

Jesus taught the people as one who had authority and not as their scribes taught them. (see Matthew 7:29) And in the same way, this was true in Paul's life and ministry.

To me, this is the most encouraging fact about Paul's life. Paul was a person very much like you and like me. When you study his life, there's hope because we can become like him. If

God could do it in Paul, He can do it in anyone. I am convinced that God gave us Paul to be an example and an encouragement.

It's so rare to find people who are real—who live out their faith in such a practical way that it's at work all the time. They seem to attract people to Christ by their very presence. When you're with them, spiritual things become natural and easy to talk about. In fact, it becomes hard to talk about anything else! They have a way of bringing you into the presence of God. Such people bear fruit everywhere they go. This is how we can be, too, as we live a life of reality.

Just as apple seeds produce apples, and pears produce pears, so we will bear spiritual fruit to the extent we understand and live out the kind of commitment to Christ that Paul did.

So it seems that in Paul, God deliberately gave us the hope that we, too, can live such a fruitful and overcoming life. In fact, Paul encourages this idea more than once.

To the Corinthians, he said, after spending one and a half years with them, "You have seen my life; follow me."

To Timothy, he said, "And the things that thou hast heard of me among many witnesses, the same commit thou to faithful men, who shall be able to teach others also." (2 Timothy 2:2)

And after spending three years with the elders at Ephesus, he tells them, "Ye know ... what manner I have been with you in all seasons. ... Take heed therefore unto yourselves ..." (Acts 20:18,28)

Chapter 28

The Secret of His Life

So what was the secret of Paul's extraordinary life? Was it his education, background, abilities, or special privileges?

No, it was nothing Paul had in himself that made it possible for him to live this life I am talking about. In Romans 7:18, he says, "For I know that in me (that is, in my flesh,) dwelleth no good thing. ..."

There was nothing, absolutely nothing, in himself that made him what he was. On the other hand, all his background and education, the prestige, and all the privileges given to him were nothing but manure in his thinking. Paul says in Philippians 3 he counted it all "as dung." It was all cancelled out in his mind. He started from zero.

Although he did have great natural and spiritual gifts, Paul never boasts or relies on them. Instead, he deliberately downplays, ignores and casts these benefits aside.

Paul seldom had any illusions about himself. He was no superstar, and he knew it. He was practical enough to write that we need to die *daily*, taking up our personal cross from moment to moment. There's no hint here of a man who feels he has "arrived." Instead, we see a man who recognizes life is a spiritual journey.

He reminded himself and others constantly that he was just an earthen vessel, an ordinary, everyday person. During Paul's life and ministry he certainly didn't fit the modern-day image of a dynamic, handsome, traveling evangelist.

In fact, he didn't exhibit much of a physical presence either. People were shocked at his tiny frame and squeaky voice. Tradition says he was only four foot, six inches tall. When he was in the market place, this little man could scarcely be seen unless he was standing on top of a rock or a box!

If he had stood behind our average pulpit today, you probably wouldn't even have seen him. He himself talks about his speech as contemptible. From other passages it is clear Paul was no great public speaker. He must have been like Moses who cried out to God, "I can't talk!"

All this tells us he was far from being a polished personality. He was an ordinary man. As a matter of fact, if Paul were to walk on today's streets, I imagine we would hardly notice him. Even if we did, we might look at him with pity—or offer to help him cross the street because he was nearly blind.

Many people believe he had poor eyesight—perhaps a disease or even cataracts. This poor eyesight must have been a constant trial. In the book of Galatians, he says, "See what large letters I use as I write ..." (Galatians 6:11, *NIV*) The problem must have been obvious and provoked pity from others for he says to them, "If it had been possible, ye would have plucked out your own eyes, and have given them to me." (Galatians 4:15)

Then, too, he had a short temper and didn't always get along well with others. How many of us can relate to this! He was a man just like us, who quarreled with his co-worker Barnabas. He was so impatient on one occasion that he had no room in his heart to forgive and accept young Mark.

Moreover, he knew he was made of dust. This is the reason why we read in 2 Corinthians 4:7-12: "But we have this treasure in earthen vessels, that the excellency of the power may be of God, and not of us. We are troubled on every side, yet not distressed; we are perplexed, but not in despair; persecuted, but not forsaken; cast down, but not destroyed; always bearing about in the body the dying of the Lord Jesus, that the life also of Jesus might be made manifest in our body. For we which live are alway delivered unto death for Jesus' sake, that the life also of Jesus may be made manifest in our mortal flesh. So then death worketh in us, but life in you."

Here we read of a man beset with the same fears, agonies and letdowns we all face. He had to handle all the emotions and struggles that any ordinary person like you and I must deal with in our daily lives. In another place, Paul talks about how he came to Corinth with fear and trembling.

Saul Before Conversion

Saul, the young man who became Paul, should be especially easy for 20th-century Christians to relate to because, in many ways, he was a 20th-century man living in the first century. Western readers, especially Americans, probably should be able to relate to Saul as well as any other character in the Bible.

Before his conversion, he lived a life quite similar to that of the average American today. He was a man of enormous privilege. Born and raised in the rich seaport of Tarsus, he enjoyed the best of all worlds. His cultural background combined Roman citizenship, Greek culture and Hebrew scholarship. One cannot imagine this youth being deprived of any material, mental or spiritual need in the way he was raised.

There is no doubt Saul was intellectually brilliant, savvy to ways of the world, and a global thinker. In an information culture where knowledge was power, young Saul was uniquely positioned. In addition, he had the right connections in Jerusalem. He had the educational and family pedigree needed to go to the top in any field.

Perhaps his small stature and fanatical religious zeal for the faith of his fathers were drawbacks in some circles, but both Roman and Jewish society would have overlooked them if Saul had played his cards right.

Young Saul appears to have been politically active, socially liberated, capable, respected and self-confident. It is not hard to imagine this idealistic young zealot being arrogant—even bigoted and hateful. He was self-righteous enough to participate in the murder of Stephen and so spiritually blind that he apparently missed the Gospel witness in Stephen's trial and martyrdom.

If God had not intervened, it is interesting to speculate on where Saul's ability, determination, intellect and zeal might have led him. It is not hard to imagine him as a powerful political leader, a judge, a general or a successful businessman. He was driven by fleshly ambition and was probably capable of achieving just about anything this world offered in his life.

You can see why Saul was so much like the average American today—affluent, ambitious, informed, religious, self-confident and sophisticated. Saul had everything, including a religious fanaticism so powerful that it sent him off to track down and destroy the early Christians.

Paul—The Broken Man

But then it happened. Saul met Jesus on the Damascus Road, and his life was changed radically. Blinded by the living God, Saul had little pride and self-confidence left as he was led by the hand to the house of Ananias.

There, as he met the Lord Jesus Christ, he asked this all-important question, which I believe was one of the most important secrets in Paul's life: "Lord, what do You want me to do?"

You see, as an ordinary, earthen vessel, Paul was just like you and me. As he met the Lord Jesus Christ, he turned over the rulership of his life to Jesus. That word, *kurios*, in the original text means "the one who has authority over, ownership." Up until then, Paul had been living for his traditions, his religion—and above all, himself, governing and running his life.

Now he threw up his hands and said, "Lord, here, take my hands and chain them to Yours. I want to be Yours now and forevermore. I am giving up the right to run my own life. From now on, You will take charge."

In other words, Paul made Jesus Christ the Lord of all in his life. I believe the only way you can ever fulfill the call of God in your life is by turning over your life and every detail, the smallest and the biggest decisions you make—all things—to the Master.

Paul explained this in 1 Corinthians 7:23: "Ye are bought with a price; be not ye the servants of men." He was no longer listening to what other people said about him—either good or bad. Now he was freed from the opinions of men.

How true it is that most of the time we are not able to live the life of Jesus in our mortal bodies because we are far too concerned about the opinions of other people. We cannot value the opinions of parents, brothers and sisters, church members or the people at work above that of the true Master, the Lord Jesus Christ. One of the first cords we must cut is the desire to be accepted, approved and understood by people around us.

Throughout the history of mankind, you will find that those who walked with the living God were often lonely men. They were misunderstood, forsaken and rejected. They knew the pain of feeling the cold wind of opposition against their face. As long as we remain tied to people's opinions about us, we can never know the power of a supernatural life. Such Christians are like a bouncing ball, now and then touching the ceiling of spirituality, maybe experiencing some joy and ecstasy in Sunday worship services but then again drawn back to the dust, feeling defeated and discouraged.

I ask then, is your commitment to the Lord Jesus Christ real enough that you are willing to count the cost of losing friendships, family ties and anything that comes between you and the Lord?

The Cost of Following Him

Jesus made it very clear that when you follow Him, your own household and even the best of friends can become your enemies. But then He does not offer anything else other than that which He faced in His life. Paul had to walk away from all things and everything that he knew. For three years alone in the desert, he became acquainted with the Master for whom he had given his life completely and totally. So he said, when he was called by the Lord, he did not consult with flesh and blood to seek others' opinions as to what he must do.

So the next question I ask is, Are you willing to do the same?

If your answer is yes, then I guarantee you have taken the first step to experience such a life. In 1 Corinthians 6:19,20, Paul says, "Know ye not that your body is the temple of the Holy Ghost which is in you, which ye have of God, and ye are not your own? For ye are bought with a price: therefore glorify God in your body ..."

This was the positive side of Paul's commitment to Christ and what made Jesus his true Lord and Master. He recognized that blood was the price Jesus paid for Paul, and he was no longer his own. For so long, he had robbed God. He had held his life back. Now, in repentance, he came and gave his life back to the Lord. Just like a bank manager who handles millions and millions of dollars but has no right to use that money for himself, so Paul realized his own life, everything in it, small and great, was no longer his. It was purchased with the blood of the Lord Jesus Christ. Based on this, he surrendered his life to become a bondslave of the Lord Jesus. His commitment now and forever was to do nothing but the will of his Master.

Chapter 29

Waiting for Orders

Often, in India, in front of office buildings, you will see a messenger boy sitting on a stool, apparently doing nothing. But when he hears a bell ringing inside, he hurries in and asks, "Sir, what do you want me to do?"

Whatever the instructions may be, he follows them without complaining. Then he returns and sits, waiting again to hear his master's voice. This is the kind of commitment God wants from us.

But this is the opposite of the mad, rushing, pragmatic, modern-day evangelical Christianity most of us are caught up in today.

Somehow we assume God is in some big mess, that we should run around and frantically take His side, or He will be in big trouble. On the other hand, I believe God is waiting for those who are willing to become bondslaves, men and women who will wait and watch to hear the Master's voice and only do those things He asks them to do.

A half hour with God, limited to doing His will in His way, is worth more than a million years doing the best in our own self and energy. All fleshly effort will be burned to ash and will not make it into eternity.

Have you recognized the fact that you are bought with a price, that you are not your own? If so, you have no right to decide even the smallest matters in your life. What kind of commitment have you made to Christ? Are you just "returning a favor" in your Christian service, or have you surrendered the totality of your life and everything in it to His control?

Are you still the one who is running around with brilliant ideas, seeking to do this and that for God? Or are you one who is so committed to Christ that you are not motivated nor persuaded by anything external? Are you dead to the voices of others, your own ego and ambitions, but alive to the voice of the Holy Spirit?

If the life of Paul has any secret for us, it is this, "For to me to live is Christ, and to die is gain." (Philippians 1:21)

There also are several areas in our lives where this truth must make an impact if we are to find the reality we seek.

Your Marriage

If you are a young person thinking of marriage, have you asked the Lord what type of person He wants you to marry? Who told you that you must date everyone you meet to test it out to make sure you are getting the right deal?

Have you ever wondered and asked whether the traditions and voices of men regarding choosing a partner are of God, or are they created by this world's corrupt system? What are you looking for in that person you want to marry? Education, money, future, abilities and talents? Or are you looking for a person who is totally committed to Christ with his or her whole heart?

You must give up your right to decide on your marriage and your life's partner. Seek the Lord with all your heart, and keep eternal values in mind as you decide about marriage. Many hundreds of godly young people have destroyed their lives and God's call upon their lives because they fell in the temptation of marrying someone based upon the external things rather than the call and voice of God in their decision.

If you already are married, what are your expectations from your mate? Have your values shifted to personal comfort, security and the things of this world since your marriage? Do you desire for your mate to do the will of God at all costs—even if it means sacrifice for you? As you pray for your husband or your wife, is the will of God number one?

Your Education

I will never forget talking to a couple who wept with much regret over the ruined Christian life of their son. He was breaking their hearts. A straight-A student as he finished high school, he at first had wanted to go and serve the Lord on the mission field.

However, his parents had been brought up to worship education. They were good, fundamental/evangelical Christian parents, but they could not see how God could use someone like him without further education. For months, the young man persisted in talking about his vision for lost souls, but his parents would not release him. He was one of those who believed he must do only those things his parents told him to do. In the end, they persuaded him to go to the pastor for counseling. Pressured by the parents, the pastor urged and convinced the young man he must go for higher education.

So, against his own heart and conscience, the boy went off to the university. In the very first year, he fell in love with a girl and married her. Two years went by, and soon he was completely backslidden, ending up divorced. Now the parents were weeping before me, having recognized how they became instruments to keep their son from following the Lord with all his heart.

I am not blaming anyone in this situation, but it makes me ask a critical question. Who told us we must have university degrees?

Millions of young people born and raised in Christian homes are going on for higher education only to discover their missionary vision ends. Rarely do they make it to the mission field. I am convinced this so-called higher education "to serve God and live for Him" is one of the greatest deceptions of our time. God is looking for those who will give their lives completely and totally, even if they have nothing in terms of education or the things of this world. Don't misunderstand me—I am not against education, nor anyone going to a college or university to get the best education possible. I am only asking, Are you pursuing what God has asked you to do? Have you submitted this area to God for Him to lead you?

Your Job

The idea that more pay and career advancement obviously must be of God is a common myth. Many believe it, but it is not true.

The real question is, Have you truly and honestly fasted and prayed for God to direct you to your job and the place where you are working?

It could be you would earn much more money elsewhere, but God wants you to be where you are! Perhaps a lower position, with less pay and less prestige, is where He wants you in order to impact that area, those people and that society for His kingdom's sake. All you do on your job might be incidental. The most important thing is that you are an ambassador, the light of the world and the salt of the earth.

God wants to place us in different places at different times for His kingdom's sake.

Of course, only those who truly seek the face of God and submit to His authority will know where He is telling them to go. The question is, have you asked Him about it? Or is that career decision, that move, that salary something you are seeking without direction from the Lord Jesus?

Do you plan to give a little bit of "your" money or time to God on the side to keep Him happy? We must destroy this kind of worldly ambition and selfish planning if we are serious about following Christ all the way. We must come back to God and submit this area to Him along with all the others.

Your Buying And Selling

We are living in a society where new catalogs by the thousands are put out every season. We are enticed to buy the latest fashions and newest products of the day. Sales deceive us into buying bargains we don't need. Our minds are so gone that we don't stop and ask God for His will about what we are going to purchase. We think we have a free right to get what we want, when we want it.

That television set you bought—did you ask God about it? Was it His will? Those new fashions, the toys, the car—no, don't misunderstand me—I am not against you buying things. What I am saying is that God is concerned about the decisions you make with your pocketbook. Is He the Lord of your buying?

Your Children

For my wife and me, even before our children were born, it was our continuous prayer every day for God to save their souls and call them to be missionaries. We pray with them and help them as they pray for themselves.

For those of us who are following Christ, is not eternity more important than time? All that we have, all that we build, all our security—everything about us—is going to be burned up. Truly we are being prepared by the living God to reign with Jesus forever throughout eternity. We are destined for the throne. If that is the case, what is your greatest wish for your children?

When was the last time you prayed and shed tears, asking God to call your children to serve Him?

Are you willing to give up your children to go to some far away country, if need be, never to return, in order to serve Him?

What is it you want for your children—the best health, the best education, the best family, the best house?

What about seeking the best for them as God wants it?

But what does God want? Of course, you will never know until you have submitted your children and your life completely to the lordship of Christ, seeking His face and asking Him daily, "Lord, what do you want us to do?"

Your Money

The traditions and wisdom of our society, and our fears for the future, still dictate what most Christians will do with their money and resources. As you look at the material things of this world, have you truly asked God what He wants you to do with these earthly goods? Jesus talked much about wealth and the things of the world. He admonished us very strongly, "Lay not up for yourselves treasures upon earth, where moth and rust doth corrupt." (Matthew 6:19) He told us to store our treasure in heaven. He told us to use unrighteous mammon to build friends for eternity; that is, to win precious souls.

Many people give their resources to God out of abundance or guilt. Are you one of them?

Or do you seek to live as simply as you can, with as little as you can on the barest of essentials, so you can send more into His work? The average Christian spends more money on dog food and lawn care than for the cause of God's kingdom because he has completely taken his life and finances away from the living God's hand. He is his own master when it comes to money and resources. He has never sought God's face and has never submitted to Him in this area as His bondslaves.

I challenge you to read throughout the New Testament and mark every verse where Jesus and the apostles talk about the riches of this world. Seek to obey the Word, not to explain it. Then see what marvelous changes will come into your life. The miracle of faith will become a reality. Have you submitted this area of your life to God?

Your Time

The amount of time the average believer spends before a television, reading worldly novels and in recreation is amazing.

Even in church, we study our watches carefully to make sure the preacher will not spend one minute more than the 25 minutes allotted for him to preach.

What a travesty! How far we have fallen when giving an hour or two a week to God is a painful exercise. One who has submitted his life to God cannot divorce time from it.

How are you spending your leisure time? Who told you to take so many weeks for vacation here or there? Who told you to read every conceivable magazine article and watch television in order to be informed? The world and its system are still run by the prince of this world, and Satan is seeking to get every minute he can out of your life.

Satan has laid a hundred little time traps to keep you from being effective for Christ.

We need to be praying for God's guidance about our vacations and Christmas and other holidays. Can this time be used for the kingdom instead of wasted selfishly?

How much time do you spend in prayer each day? It is shocking to know that the average choir member who sings in our churches spends more time practicing his or her voice and instruments than in reading God's Word and in prayer.

If we were submitting our time to the will of Christ, how would our lives differ? Who is lord of your time? Do you consider it your own, or do you ask the Lord for His plans for your minutes, hours and days?

Yet we find in the lives of Jesus and Paul—and those who follow them today—that every minute is submitted to doing the will of God.

Your Private Life

One of the greatest tragedies of this civilized, modern society is that people are told—and they have come to believe it—that no one has anything to say about his or her private life. No one should intrude, and no one should disturb.

But there is no such thing for the Christian. So my question is simple, Have you submitted your so-called private world to the lordship of Christ?

What about the places you go, the things you read and the people you talk to, your telephone conversations, the magazines you buy, the movies you watch, the friendships you keep?

For so many Christians, their inner man has been destroyed and lays in shambles—all because it has never been submitted to the authority of God. Such believers insist they are their own masters; hence, they live this earthly life defeated and destroyed by the powers of darkness. What about you?

I believe Paul was a man who looked at each area of his life and said, "Lord, here I am. What do you want me to do?"

Again and again, as the Lord put more light on his life, we see Paul repenting and walking the way of the cross. After 20 years of preaching, he confessed he was the chief of sinners, the least of the least of the brethren. In Philippians 3:12-14, he says boldly that he considers himself "not as though I ... were already perfect. ... but this one thing I do, forgetting those things which are behind, and reaching forth unto those things which are before, I press toward the mark for the prize of the high calling of God in Christ Jesus."

How did Paul and others like him keep going with this kind of life?

I believe it is only possible through continuous self-examination and confession. We need to compare our lifestyles repeatedly against Scripture. Then, seeing where we need to be, we repent, get up and go on!

Often I have to get on my face and say, "Lord, again I have failed. You are right, and I want to go on. Please forgive me and cleanse me."

This must be a daily practice. And I have to do it in so many areas of my own life.

The beautiful thing is this: When Jesus died on the cross, He forgave all the sin you ever committed, are committing, and will commit.

Before the prodigal son came home, his father had forgiven him. His agony and the memorized prayer he recited were not what motivated his father to forgive him. It was the very nature of the father to forgive. If, when we were enemies, God loved us this much, how much more does He love us when we have responded to Him and now are His children?

Some of the greatest verses in the New Testament for me are Romans 8:32-39.

Read this slowly and prayerfully. "He that spared not his own Son, but delivered him up for us all, how shall he not with him also freely give us all things? Who shall lay any thing to the charge of God's elect? It is God that justifieth. Who is he that condemneth? It is Christ that died, yea rather, that is risen again, who is even at the right hand of God, who also maketh intercession for us. Who shall separate us from the love of Christ? Shall tribulation, or distress, or persecution, or famine, or nakedness, or peril, or sword? As it is written, For thy sake we are killed all the day long; we are accounted as sheep for the slaughter. Nay, in all these things we are more than conquerors through him that loved us. For I am persuaded, that neither death, nor life, nor angels, nor principalities, nor powers, nor things present, nor things to come, nor height, nor depth, nor any other creature, shall be able to separate us from the love of God, which is in Christ Jesus our Lord."

His Grace Is Sufficient

As we have come to the end of this book, let me say that the most important key to remember in such a life of following Christ is continuous repentance when we fall short. Keep a short account with God; and His grace is sufficient.

Remember, only those soldiers who go to the battlefield get shot at and wounded. Those who stay home and take it easy never know the struggle of fighting with the enemy. As you launch out now by faith to follow the Lord in His footsteps, you are to take up the armor of God. You have plunged into the very heat of the battle. You are in the enemy's camp, and you cannot turn back.

One of the most subtle tactics the enemy tries is to make you ineffective by discouraging you and causing you to sin.

In the Old Testament, when the enemy of God's people wanted to defeat Israel, they asked Balaam what to do. Balaam told them to entice God's people into sin. That is exactly what they did and, of course, Israel was defeated.

The deceitfulness of sin will keep you from achieving a committed life. When you recognize this, you must immediately repent, take God's grace and forgiveness already given to you and then thank Him for His goodness.

Remember, we are called to be soldiers. He is on our side. He loves us always, in spite of all our failures, and He wants to make us into the image of His Son. For this He has called you. Don't give up.

A Prayer

Dear Lord, we acknowledge that our commitment to You is so shallow. We say we love You, but our actions betray us.

Open our eyes so that we see time and eternity as You see them. Forgive us for forgetting we are only strangers and pilgrims on this earth.

How foolish we are, O Lord, to store up treasures on this earth and fight to save our lives and preserve them, when You tell us we will lose our lives if we try to do that.

We ask You, dear Lord, to forgive us and help us to walk in Your footsteps—forsaking all, denying ourselves, carrying our crosses daily and loving You supremely so Your causes might be furthered in this dark and dying world.

In Jesus' name, Amen.

 GOSPEL FOR ASIA

You Can Become a Sender!

Yes! **I will help support a native missionary**, reaching his own people for as little as $30 (£20) a month. It takes from $90-$150 US ($120-$180 CDN, £40-£80 UK) to fully support a missionary, including family support and ministry expenses.

To begin sponsoring today call toll free:
1-800-WIN-ASIA
(1-800-946-2742)

In Canada, call 1-888-WIN-ASIA.

Or complete this form and mail it to Gospel for Asia:
In the US: 1800 Golden Trail Court, Carrollton, TX 75010
Canada: 245 King Street E, Stoney Creek, ON   L8G 1L9
UK: PO Box 19, Bognor Regis, West Sussex PO22 7UD

❏ **Starting now, I will prayerfully support** _____ native missionaries at $30 (£20) each per month = $_____ a month.

You'll receive a photo and testimony
of each native missionary you help sponsor.

❏ **Please send me more information** about how to help sponsor a native missionary, including a one-year FREE subscription to *Send!*—the voice of native missions.

Please circle: Mr. Mrs. Miss Rev.

Name _____

Address _____

City _____ State/PR/County _____ Zip/PC _____

Country _____ Phone (____) _____

HA14-RB2S   ZHR4-RB2S   YHR4-RB2S

 Gospel for Asia sends 100% of your missionary support to the mission field. Nothing is taken out for administrative expenses. All donations are tax deductible as allowed by law.

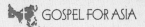 GOSPEL FOR ASIA

Help Us Involve Others

Give your Christian friends and relatives a FREE subscription to *Send!*—the voice of native missions. Help give them a missions vision! Just fill out their names and addresses below. Use additional sheets of paper if necessary. Please print clearly.

Please circle: Mr.   Mrs.   Miss   Rev.

Name _____

Address _____

City _____   State/PR/County _____   Zip/PC _____

Country _____   Phone (___) _____

Please circle: Mr.   Mrs.   Miss   Rev.

Name _____

Address _____

City _____   State/PR/County _____   Zip/PC _____

Country _____   Phone (___) _____

FA14-PB2Ø   ZFR4-PB2Ø   YFR4-PB2Ø

❏ Please identify me as the gift subscription donor.
My name is: _____

GOSPEL FOR ASIA   ECFA CHARTER MEMBER

Mail to:
United States:
Gospel for Asia, 1800 Golden Trail Court, Carrollton, TX 75010

Canada:
Gospel for Asia, 245 King Street E, Stoney Creek, ON   L8G 1L9

United Kingdom:
Gospel for Asia, PO Box 19, Bognor Regis, West Sussex, PO22 7UD

Other Challenging Books
by K.P. Yohannan

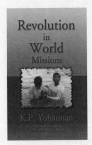

Revolution in World Missions

This book tells how the Lord used a young Indian boy named K.P. Yohannan to begin a major revolution to win Asia to Christ. Filled with powerful examples of commitment and sacrifice, it demonstrates the effectiveness of native missionaries.

Suggested donation: $3 US/$3 CDN/£3 UK
Order code: B1

Also Available on Audiocassette:
Suggested donation: $9 US/$12 CDN/£6 UK
Order code: B1AC

Reflecting His Image

K.P. Yohannan takes us on a journey back to God's original purpose for each of our lives: to reflect His image. This book is a compilation of short, easy-to-read chapters that all deal with following Christ closely.

Suggested donation: $8 US/$10 CDN/£4.50 UK
Order code: B5

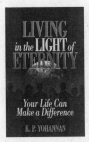

Living in the Light of Eternity

K.P. Yohannan lovingly, yet candidly, reminds Christians of their primary role while here on earth: harvesting souls. This book challenges us to look at our heart attitudes, motivation and our impact on eternity.

Suggested donation: $8 US/$10 CDN/£4.50 UK
Order code: B4

Also Available on Audiocassette:
Suggested donation: $9 US/$12 CDN/£6 UK
Order code: B4AC

Videos and Other Materials

Glad Sacrifice

This exciting 23-minute video shows real-life native missionaries spreading the Gospel across Asia. As you watch these dramatic scenes you will rejoice in God's plan to reach Asia for Christ.

Suggested donation: $6 US/$8 CDN/£8.50 UK
Order code: V3

Christ's Call: "Follow My Footsteps"

In this compelling 41-minute video, K.P. Yohannan challenges us to follow in Christ's footsteps—steps that will deliver us from our self-centeredness and cause us to impact the lost millions in our generation.

Suggested donation: $6 US/$8 CDN/£8.50 UK
Order code: V1

Operation Boot Camp

This 15-minute video will transport you to India and take you inside one of Gospel for Asia's intensive training centers. Learn why the training is so challenging. Meet young men who are willing to lay down their lives to reach the unreached of Asia.

Suggested donation: $6 US/$8 CDN/£8.50 UK
Order code: V4

World Map

Allow God to burden your heart for the lost with GFA's *Pray for the World* laminated map.

Wall Map: 21.5 x 36 inches
Suggested donation: $8 US/$11 CDN/£5 UK
Order Code: **MAPL**

Placemat-sized Map: 11 x 18 inches
Suggested donation: $3 US/£2.5 UK
Order Code: **MAPM**

Built on the Solid Rock

This 15-minute video documents how Gospel for Asia's church-planting ministry is exploding across previously unreached areas of the *10/40 Window*. See lives being transformed for eternity as people turn to Christ.

Suggested donation: $6 US/$8 CDN/£8.50 UK
Order code: V6

Seek Only God's Approval

In this 56-minute video K.P. offers no shortcuts to spritual success. He simply demonstrates from the Word of God that true Christianity is a call to all-out commitment, without reservation. Others have walked this road before us, and their lives testify that the living God is indeed able and willing to make us more fruitful than we could ever imagine.

Suggested donation: $6 US/$8 CDN/£8.50 UK
Order code: V7

On Tour with Brother K. P.

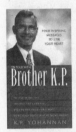

Here is an audiocassette series that will challenge and inspire you. This package contains four of K.P.'s best-loved messages delivered in churches across the United States.

Suggested donation: $9 US/$12 CDN/£6 UK
Order code: CS1

Window to our World

This missions unit study has been created to help children and their families make an eternal impact upon a lost and dying world, and take an active part in fulfilling the Great Commission. The Unit Study Packet consists of a Teacher's Manual and four 16 to 20-page units, each profiling a different country in the *10/40 Window*. Every unit is specially designed to inspire the hearts of children ages 8 to 14 to follow Jesus in making disiples of all nations.

Suggested donation for Unit Study Packet: $12 US/$15 CDN/£8 UK
Order code: WOW1

Order Form

 GOSPEL FOR ASIA

Code	Quantity	Donation
B1 *(EXAMPLE)*	2 *(EXAMPLE)*	$6.00 *(EXAMPLE)*

US Postage enclosed*:	US ONLY
CDN Postage enclosed**:	CDN ONLY
Additional donation for native missionaries:	
TOTAL DONATION ENCLOSED:	

*US Postage: 1-4 items—$1 per item; 5-10 items—75¢ per item; 11+ items—10%
**Canadian Postage: 1-3 items—$5; 4-8 items—$6; 9-14 items—$7; 15+ items—add 25¢ per item

Please circle: Mr.   Mrs.   Miss   Rev.

Name _____

Address _____

City _____ State/PR/County _____ Zip/PC _____

Country _____ Phone ( )_____

Mail Order to: HA14-PLF2   ZHR4-PLF2   YHR4-PLF2

United States: Literature Department, Gospel for Asia, 1800 Golden Trail Court, Carrollton, TX 75010; **Or phone:** 1-800-WIN-ASIA (946-2742)

Canada: Gospel for Asia, 245 King Street E, Stoney Creek, ON   L8G 1L9 **Or phone:** 1-888-WIN-ASIA (946-2742)

United Kingdom: Gospel for Asia, PO Box 19, Bognor Regis, West Sussex, PO22 7UD

Or visit us online:
www.gfa.org

Make all checks payable to GOSPEL FOR ASIA. Please allow two to three weeks for delivery. All gifts to Gospel for Asia are tax deductible less the fair market value of the materials you receive from us. The suggested donations are at or below the fair market value of each item and are subject to change.

 ECFA CHARTER MEMBER